T0278284

The 500 Hidden Secrets of

TOKYO

INTRODUCTION

___

Japan is supposed to be a monolingual and monocultural country. Take a closer look at it on a map however, and you will discover that it actually consists of a group of several islands. The country has many different cultural characteristics, depending on the regions. There are hundreds of accents which might be too different from one another to be considered dialects.

Tokyo, the country's capital, is a microcosm of Japan, attracting people from all over the country. What do you see in your mind when you think of Tokyo? A city in manga and anime? A city filled with high-tech gadgets? A city where people bow frequently even when they are on the phone? The truth is that, as a city, Tokyo is a bit of a mish-mash with many different combinations. A tall futuristic building is built alongside an old house. A boy wearing clothes from the latest collection of a French brand walks hand-in-hand with a girl in a traditional kimono.

You might also think of Tokyo as one of the most crowded cities in the world. Don't let that scare you: it's true. Tokyo is very densely populated, but there is so much more to it. It has a great many aspects that are changing at a rapid pace; hopefully *The 500 Hidden Secrets of Tokyo* will help you discover new sides to this city that you were unaware of, and will inspire you as you organise your holiday here.

HOW TO
USE THIS BOOK?

———

This guide lists 500 things you need to know about Tokyo in 100 different categories. Most of these are places to visit, with practical information to help you find your way. Others are bits of information that help you get to know the city and its habitants. The aim of this guide is to inspire, not to cover the city from A to Z.

The places listed in the guide are given an address – please note that first floor is ground floor in Japan – including the neighbourhood, and a number. The neighbourhood and number allow you to find the locations on the maps at the beginning of the book: first look for the map of the corresponding neighbourhood, then look for the right number. A word of caution: these maps are not detailed enough to allow you to find specific locations in the city. You can obtain an excellent map from any tourist office or in most hotels. Or the addresses can be located on a smartphone.

Please also bear in mind that cities change all the time. The chef who hits a high note one day may be uninspiring on the day you happen to visit. The hotel ecstatically reviewed in this book might suddenly go downhill under a new manager. The bar considered one of the 5 must-visit bars in Shinjuku Golden-Gai might be empty on the night you visit. This is obviously a highly personal selection. You might not always agree with it. If you want to leave a comment, recommend a bar or reveal your favourite secret place, please visit the website *the500hiddensecrets.com* – you'll also find free tips and the latest news about the series there – or follow *@500hiddensecrets* on Instagram or Facebook and leave a comment.

THE AUTHOR

Yukiko Tajima was born and raised in Tokyo. In her mid-20s, she decided she wanted to see another part of the world – not just as a tourist but to live there. And so she moved to the UK. After living there for seven years in the 1990s, she started to rediscover and appreciate her own culture more than ever. Since then she has been involved in many different projects to promote Japanese culture abroad.

Yukiko Tajima now lives in the heart of Tokyo, which is visited by tourists from all over the world throughout the year. As a local, she started wondering whether these tourists have access to all of the available information. Thanks to today's technology, including smartphone apps and online translators, travelling by yourself in a city where you do not understand the language has become much easier, but that still doesn't mean that everyone can find out everything there is to know. That is why Yukiko Tajima wrote this book: she hopes that it will allow people to get to know Tokyo a bit better than they do now. She herself now is, after writing this book, prouder of her city than she ever was.

The author would like to thank all her friends who helped gather the addresses. She also wants to thank Luster Publishing for giving her the opportunity to discover things about Tokyo that she didn't know yet. Last but not least, she thanks Tinne Luyten, because without her, she would never have found out about this excellent series of guidebooks.

N° DISTRICT — Area name

① SHIBUYA-KU — Shibuya

② SHIBUYA-KU / MEGURO-KU — Daikanyama, Ebisu, Hiroo and Nakameguro

③ SHIBUYA-KU — Harajuku

④ MINATO-KU — Aoyama

⑤ MINATO-KU / SHINJUKU-KU — Akasaka, Yotsuya and Ichigaya

⑥ MINATO-KU — Azabu, Roppongi and Hiroo

⑦ SHINJUKU-KU — Yoyogi and Shinjuku

⑧ CHIYODA-KU / CHUO-KU — Ginza and Nihonbashi

⑨ CHIYODA-KU — Kanda

⑩ BUNKYO-KU / TAITO-KU — Ueno and Asakusa

⑪ TOSHIMA-KU — Ikebukuro and Waseda

⑫ NAKANO-KU / SUGINAMI-KU — Tokyo West

⑬ SETAGAYA-KU — Setagaya

⑭ SHINAGAWA-KU / OTA-KU — Tokyo South

⑮ SUMIDA-KU / KOTO-KU — Tokyo East

TOKYO

overview districts

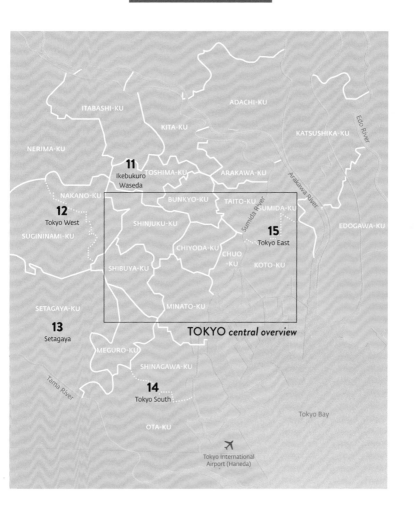

TOKYO

central overview

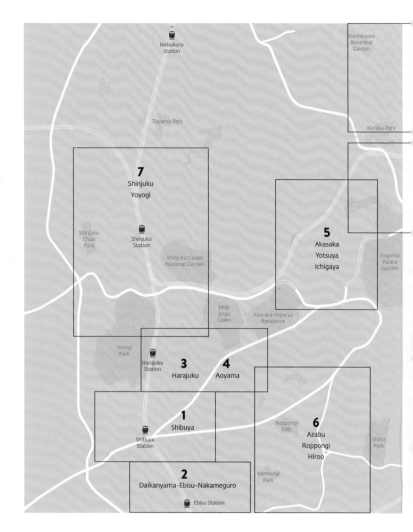

Ikebukuro Station

Koishikawa Botanical Garden

Toyama Park

Koraku Park

7
Shinjuku
Yoyogi

Shinjuku Chuo Park

Shinjuku Station

5
Akasaka
Yotsuya
Ichigaya

Imperial Palace Garden

Shinjuku Gyoen National Garden

Meiji Jingu Gaien

Akasaka Imperial Residence

Yoyogi Park

Harajuku Station

3
Harajuku

4
Aoyama

1
Shibuya

Roppongi Hills

6
Azabu
Roppongi
Hiroo

Shiba Park

Shibuya Station

2
Daikanyama-Ebisu-Nakameguro

Memorial Park

Ebisu Station

EAT — **DRINK** — SHOP — BUILDINGS — DISCOVER — **CULTURE** — CHILDREN — SLEEP — WEEKEND — RANDOM

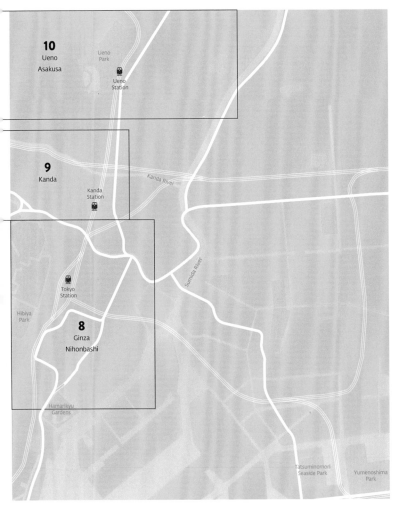

10
Ueno
Asakusa

Ueno
Park

Ueno
Station

9
Kanda

Kanda
Station

Kanda River

Sumida River

Tokyo
Station

Hibiya
Park

8
Ginza
Nihonbashi

Hamarikyu
Gardens

Tatsuminomori
Seaside Park

Yumenoshima
Park

Map 1
SHIBUYA-KU
Shibuya

Map 2

SHIBUYA-KU / MEGURO-KU

Daikanyama, Ebisu, Hiroo and Nakameguro

Map 3
SHIBUYA-KU
Harajuku

Map 4
MINATO-KU
Aoyama

Akasaka Imperial Residence

Aoyama-itchōme Station

Gaiemmae Station

Aoyama Park

Nogizaka Station

Tokyo Metropolitan Aoyama Park South District

385
292
447
171
239
238
115
211
291
150
201
187
226
281
65
193
21
191
288
29
346
206
352

Map 5

MINATO-KU / SHINJUKU-KU

Akasaka, Yotsuya and Ichigaya

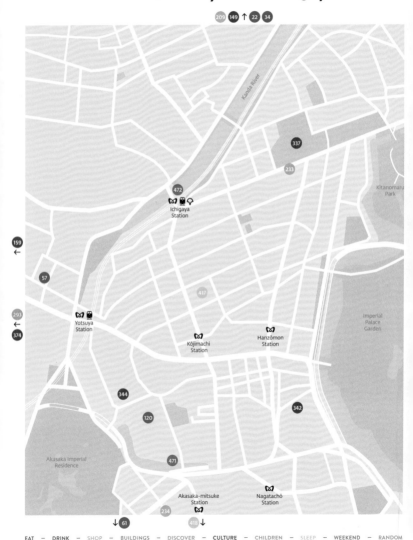

209 149 ↑ 22 34

337

233

472

Ichigaya
Station

Kitanomaru
Park

159
←

57

417

293
←
374

Yotsuya
Station

Kōjimachi
Station

Hanzōmon
Station

Imperial
Palace
Garden

344

120

342

Akasaka Imperial
Residence

471

Akasaka-mitsuke
Station

Nagatachō
Station

234

410 ↓

↓ 61

EAT — DRINK — SHOP — BUILDINGS — DISCOVER — CULTURE — CHILDREN — SLEEP — WEEKEND — RANDOM

Map 6
MINATO-KU
Azabu, Roppongi and Hiroo

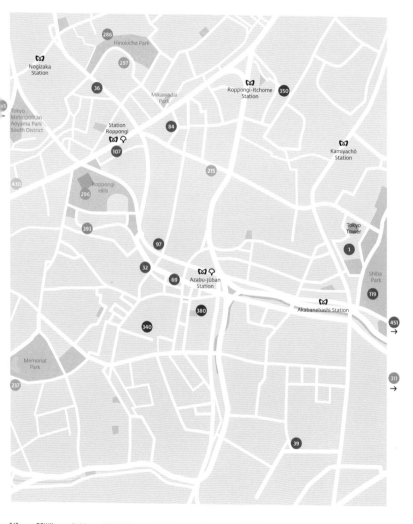

Map 7
SHINJUKU-KU
Yoyogi and Shinjuku

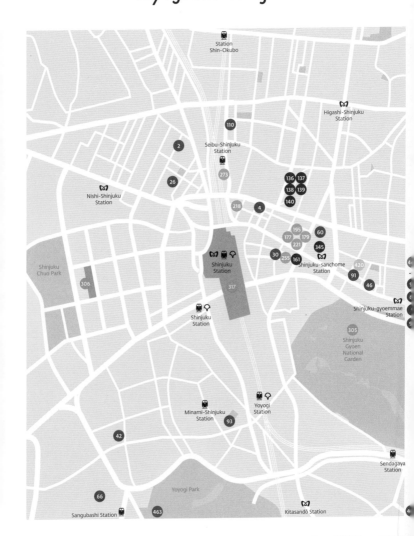

Map 8

CHIYODA-KU / CHUO-KU

Ginza and Nihonbashi

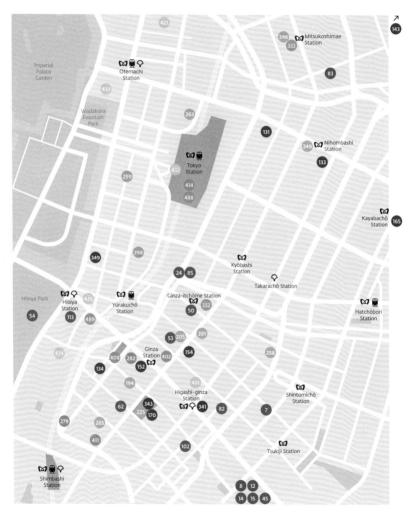

Map 9
CHIYODA-KU
Kanda

Kanda River

3

Ochanomizu
Station

434
27

Shin-Ochanomizu
Station

Awaji
Park

31

Ogawa
Hiroba

Ogawamachi
Station

Awajichō
Station

Kanda
Station

143

Map 10

BUNKYO-KU / TAITO-KU

Ueno and Asakusa

Uguisudani
Station

Iriya
Station

Tokyo
National Museum
Hyokeikan

407

naka
etery

44

429

10

376

63

Asakusa
Station

Ueno
Park

204

Ueno
Station

469   88

372 412

284

Keisei Ueno
Station

229   Station
Asakusa

Inaricho
Station

Tawaramachi
Station

Sumida River

240

Hirokoji
tion

Okachimachi
Station

Naka-Okachimachi
Station

419

↓ 264

Map 11
TOSHIMA-KU
Ikebukuro and Waseda

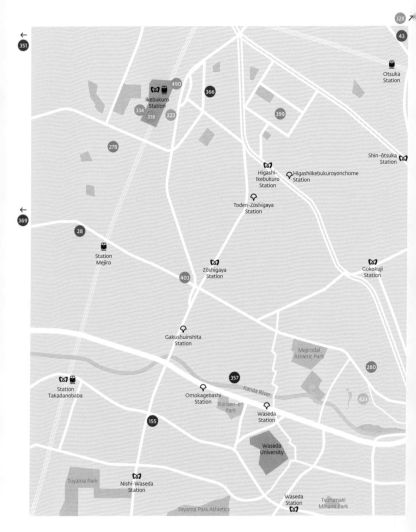

EAT — **DRINK** — SHOP — BUILDINGS — DISCOVER — **CULTURE** — CHILDREN — SLEEP — **WEEKEND** — RANDOM

Map 12

NAKANO-KU / SUGINAMI-KU

Tokyo West

Araiyakushi-mae Station

389

Ochiai Station

Mabashi Park

370

220 40

75

Higashi-Nakano Station

Kōenji Station

Nakano Station

199

Shin-Kōenji Station

Higashi-Kōenji Station

Shin-Nakano Station

Nakano-sakaue Station

371

Nishi-Shinjuku Station

Kanda River

Yanaka Park

Shinjuku Chūo Park

Seibi Park

Zenpukuji River

Wadabori Park

160

Kanda River

Eifukuchō Station

202

Yoyogi Ōyama Park

Yoyogi-Hachiman Station

Yoyogi-Uehara Station

72

Yoyogi Park

322

Meidaimae Station

235

198 252

477

Komaba Park

Shimo-Kitazawa Station

422

EAT – **DRINK** – SHOP – BUILDINGS – DISCOVER – **CULTURE** – CHILDREN – SLEEP – **WEEKEND** – RANDOM

Map 13
SETAGAYA-KU
Setagaya

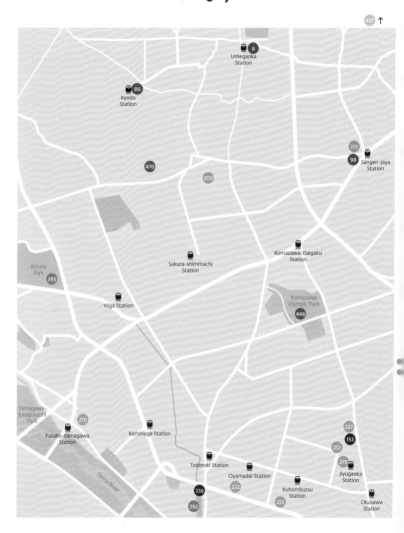

Umegaoka Station — 6

Kyodo Station — 86

470

203

310
98 — Sangen-jaya Station

Komazawa-Daigaku Station

Sakura-shimmachi Station

Kinuta Park
395

Komazawa Olympic Park
446

Yōga Station

Tamagawa-futagobashi Park

210
Futako-tamagawa Station

Kaminoge Station

227
153
212
275
Jiyugaoka Station

Tama River

Todoroki Station

Oyamadai Station

Kuhombutsu Station

336

392

232

213

Okusawa Station

Map 14
SHINAGAWA-KU / OTA-KU
Tokyo South

Map 15
SUMIDA-KU / KOTO-KU
Tokyo East

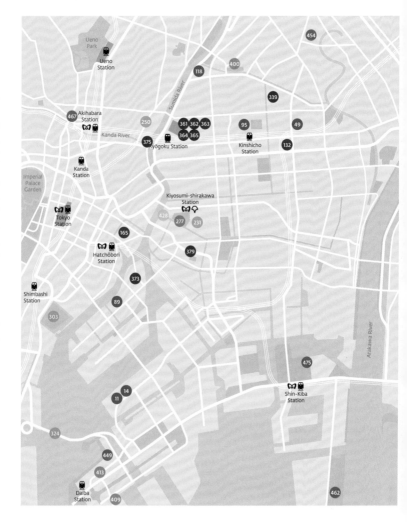

KANDA MATSUYA

風　邪やせき……
午後　六時閉店……
臨時営業のお知らせ

……

手打ちそば……一〇五〇円

すもじ　三五〇円

……三五〇円

120 PLACES TO EAT OR BUY GOOD FOOD

---

5 great **KAISEKI** and **JAPANESE** restaurants —— 34

5 **INEXPENSIVE SUSHI** restaurants —————— 36

5 great places to eat **FRESH FISH** ————— 38

5 things you need to know
BEFORE EATING SUSHI ————————— 40

The 5 best restaurants for
REGIONAL CUISINE ————————————— 42

The 5 best places for **TEMPURA** ————————— 44

The 5 best places for **JAPANESE NOODLES** —— 47

5 great places for **RAMEN** ———————————— 49

The 5 best places for **ONIGIRI** (rice balls) ————— 51

5 great **GYOZA RESTAURANTS** ————————— 53

The 5 best places to eat
JAPANESE-STYLE CURRY ————————— 55

5 must-visit restaurants for **MEAT LOVERS** —— 57

The 5 best shops for **SHAVED ICE** —— 59

5 superb **ICE-CREAM** parlours —— 62

The 5 best **BAKERIES** —— 64

5 **JAPANESE SNACKS** you should try —— 66

5 places to eat **EGG DISHES** —— 68

The 5 best places for **OKONOMIYAKI** and **MONJAYAKI** —— 70

The 5 best places for other **ASIAN CUISINE** —— 72

5 places you should go for **LATIN-AMERICAN CUISINE** —— 74

5 places to go for **A SATISFYING TAKEAWAY** — 76

5 restaurants **WHEN TIRED OF JAPANESE CUISINE** —— 78

The 5 best **VEGETARIAN** restaurants —— 80

5 nice restaurants **WITH A VIEW** —— 82

5 great
KAISEKI *and* JAPANESE
restaurants

1 **TOFUYA UKAI**
   4-4-13 Shiba Koen
   Minato-ku ⑥
   +81 (0)3-3436-1028
   ukai.co.jp

At the foot of Tokyo Tower, you can enjoy a full course tofu meal while gazing at a gorgeous Japanese garden. The tofu served at this restaurant is made in Hachioji, using exquisite water. They also serve a comprehensive selection of sakes that pair nicely with your meal.

1 TOFUYA UKAI

2 KIKUURA

7-16-3 Nishi-Shinjuku
Shinjuku-ku ⑦
+81 (0)3-5389-5581
kikuura.com

A small restaurant that serves superb meals at reasonable prices. If you go there at lunch, you can also order *donburi* (a bowl of rice with a topping) at an even more reasonable price. Bag a seat at the counter so you can watch the chef at work in the open kitchen.

3 MYOJINSHITA KANDAGAWA

2-5-11 Soto-Kanda
Chiyoda-ku ⑨
+81 (0)3-3251-5031

Eating *unagi* (freshwater eel) has been a custom in Tokyo since the Edo period. This is one of a handful of restaurants that can trace its history back to 1800. Here everything is cooked to order, meaning you will need to wait 20 minutes before you can tuck into your food, but it IS so worth the wait. Enjoy the incredible building too.

4 KURUMAYA BEKKAN

3-21-1 Shinjuku
Shinjuku-ku ⑦
+81 (0)3-3352-5566
kuruma-ya.co.jp

This restaurant used to be a salon for authors during the Showa Period. On the ground floor, they serve *teppanyaki*. *Sukiyaki* (beef and vegetables cooked in soy sauce, sake, and sugar), *shabu shabu* (thinly-sliced beef and vegetables boiled in water) and other Japanese dishes are served upstairs.

5 KUON

AT: LA REINE EBISU,
4TH FL.
1-14-15 Ebisu-Minami
Shibuya-ku ②
+81 (0)50-3198-7091
ku-on.com

A quiet and cosy restaurant on a back street in this busy area. It may also be the perfect place to celebrate your anniversary as the price/quality ratio of their meals is outstanding. They also have an *à la carte* menu (*a-ra-ka-ru-to* in Japanese) that changes every month.

5
INEXPENSIVE SUSHI
restaurants

---

6 **SUSHI NO MIDORI**
1-20-7 Umegaoka
Setagaya-ku ⑬
+81 (0)3-3429-0066
sushinomidori.co.jp

One of the most popular sushi restaurants in Tokyo, with branches in Shibuya, Ginza and other locations. Their signature *Ganso Anago* is a whole conger eel on top of rice. You can check in online so you can go shopping while waiting for your turn instead of having to queue.

7 **TSUKIJI TAMA SUSHI**
1-9-4 Tsukiji
Chuo-ku ⑧
+81 (0)3-3541-1917
tamasushi.co.jp

Since this place opened in Tsukiji in 1924, they have always had a reputation for quality sushi and service. At lunchtime, you can enjoy a set sushi menu, a bowl of Tsukiji-don, or *chirashi-sushi* at a reasonable price. Do try the *uni* (sea urchin, pronounced as 'oo-nee') if you have a chance.

8 **TSUKIJI SUSHISAY**
4-13-19 Tsukiji
Chuo-ku ⑧
+81 (0)3-351-7720
tsukijisushisay.co.jp

They have been serving affordable quality sushi here since 1889! Go for *omakase* (the chef selects toppings for you) if you are unsure what to order, or *chirashi* sushi on the upper floor. Tsukuji Sishay has several branches in Tokyo, including in Ginza, Shibuya, and Shinjuku. Takeout available.

9 MANGETSU

4-6-10 Yotsuya
Shinjuku-ku ⑦
+81 (0)3-5379-8808
*sushimangetsu-
yotsuya.com*

The ambience at this restaurant, which is located just a short walk from Yotsuya 4-chome intersection and Shinjuku Gyoen, is so relaxed that you will always feel comfortable, even if you're dining alone. Of course, you can order *nigiri* and *chirashi,* but why not try a *donburi* dish with a seasonal sashimi topping?

10 468

3-23-14 Nishi-Asakusa
Taito-ku ⑩
+81 (0)3-3843-6964

Their name is pronounced as 'yoroppa', which is the Japanese word for 'Europe'. This small sushi restaurant has only six seats and serves *bo-sushi* or 'loaf' sushi. This is prepared by layering fish and rice in a long, thin wooden box. You can also order takeaway by phone.

5 great places to eat
FRESH FISH

11 **SUSHI DAI**
AT: TOYOSU MARKET,
3RD FL.
6-5-1 Toyosu
Koto-ku ⑮
+81 (0)3-6633-0042

They are very particular here about the soy sauce and salt they use, carefully choosing the types that they believe are most suitable for sushi. Open from 5 am till 3 pm on market days. They might not serve you if you arrive just before closing time.

12 **TSUKIJI DONBURI ICHIBA**
AT: TSUKIJI MARKET
4-9-5 Tsukiji
Chuo-ku ⑧
+81 (0)3-6630-9807

While *donburi* means 'bowl', it often refers to a bowl of cooked rice topped with something. Popular dishes here include *Ichiba-don*, aka Market bowl, with sashimi on top, and *Maguro no hohoniku-don*, with grilled tuna cheek. On some weekdays, they are open 24 hours.

13 **ISONOYA (ISO-ZUSHI)**
AT: TOYOSU MARKET,
3RD FL.
6-5-1 Toyosu
Koto-ku ⑮
+81 (0)3-6633-0006
gavb701.gorp.jp

One of the popular sushi restaurants that moved here from Tsukiji Market. The place to go if you want to sample the best quality tuna in Tokyo. They serve other tasty *sashimi* as well of course. And finally, they have an English menu, which is good news if you don't read Japanese.

14 **DAIWA SUSHI**
   AT: TOYOSU MARKET
   6-3-2 Toyosu
   Koto-ku ⑮
   +81 (0)3-6633-0220

A sushi restaurant on the ground floor of the fruit and vegetable market. You should definitely order *omakase* (I leave it up to you), which is seven pieces selected by the chef. You may still feel peckish afterwards, in which case you can always order more.

15 **KANNO**
   AT: TSUKIJI MARKET
   4-9-5 Tsukiji
   Chuo-ku ⑧
   +81 (0)3-3541-9291

Another shop that serves rice bowls. Their prices have remained unchanged since they opened, so if you are looking for some affordable nosh (most of the restaurants in Tsukiji are relatively inexpensive), then try this place. Their signature dish is *Sanshu-mori*, or rice topped with tuna, salmon roe, and sea urchin.

5 things you need to know
BEFORE
EATING SUSHI

---

16 EDO-MAE STYLE

There are several styles of sushi. The *Edo-mae* style (Tokyo-style) – with raw fish scattered on top of rice – is probably the style that is most widely known as sushi outside of Japan. *Edokko* (a Japanese term referring to people born and raised in Edo, or Tokyo) tend to be impatient. So, this style suits them to a tee as the rice and fish can be eaten at the same time.

18 USE YOUR FINGERS

17 **GARI**

Gari is thinly-sliced pickled ginger. It has an antimicrobial effect, so it may prevent us from having food poisoning. It is used to cleanse the palate between eating different pieces of sushi. The word *gari* is only used for sushi ginger. The proper Japanese word for ginger is *shoga*.

18 **USE YOUR FINGERS**

Eating *Edo-mae* style sushi the proper way means you should use your fingers, not chopsticks. Grab your sushi with your thumb, index and middle fingers, turn it upside down, dip the fish into the soy sauce and eat it in one go.

19 **HOW TO ORDER**

You should start by ordering something light, like plaice or another white fish or squid, and then oily fish, like tuna or conger eel. Ultimately, you can order whatever you feel like. If you start with oily fish, you can cleanse your palate with some *gari* and green tea.

20 **DON'T WEAR PERFUME**

If you decide to go to a proper sushi restaurant – not the conveyer belt type – then don't wear perfume or only dab on the tiniest amount. The scent of perfume can easily spoil sushi. This rule also applies to other places, like sake bars for example.

The 5 best restaurants for
REGIONAL CUISINE

---

21 BOUYOUROU
5-4-41 Minami
Aoyama
Minato-ku ④
+81 (0)3-6427-2918
*aoyama-
bouyourou.com*

Fukui, one of the prefectures in Hokuriku region, is famous for its excellent seafood. At this restaurant, you can enjoy good quality raw fish and sweet shrimp. In winter, order their superb *Echizen* crab. If you're not that keen on sashimi, order Wakasa beef or 100% buckwheat *soba* noodles.

22 HONKE ABEYA
AT: CO & CO BUILDING B1
3-2-4 Kagurazaka
Shinjuku-ku ⑤
+81 (0)50-3116-0664
honkeabeya.com

Here you can eat *Hinai-Jidori*, or the chicken they raise in Akita and which is considered to be one of the top three chicken breeds. Their *Oyako-don*, or chicken and egg bowl, comes highly recommended. As Akita is a rice-producing area, it also produces good sake, which you can, of course, taste here.

23 YANMO
5-5-25 Minami-
Aoyama
Minato-ku ④
+81 (0)3-5466-0636
yanmo.co.jp

From sashimi to grilled fish, this place serves fish from the Izu Peninsula, Shizuoka. During the lunch hour, your fish is served with a bowl of rice, miso soup, and a side dish, all of which are delicious. All you can eat!

24 TOSA DINING OKYAKU

AT: THE ORB PREMIERE,
2ND FL.

**1-3-13 Ginza
Chuo-ku** ⑧
+81 (0)3-3538-4351
*marugotokochi.com/
okyaku*

There are many *antena shoppu* (shops that sell the specialities of a particular prefecture) in Ginza. This restaurant is in Kochi's shop and serves the regional dishes of Kochi, a prefecture that has plenty of seafood. Enjoy *katsuo no tataki* (lightly-broiled skipjack tuna). They also have delicious pork and beef dishes.

25 D47 SHOKUDO

AT: SHIBUYA HIKARIE,
8TH FL.

**2-21-1 Shibuya
Shibuya-ku** ①
+81 (0)3-6427-2303
d-department.com

In Japan, there are 47 prefectures. You can enjoy specialities from all over the country at this restaurant. They have a variety of *teishoku* (set menus) that change every month. They regularly organise food-related events and workshops so you can learn more about regional cuisine.

The 5 best places for
T E M P U R A

---

26   TENHIDE

7-12-21 Nishi-Shinjuku
Shinjuku-ku ⑦
+81 (0)3-5386-3630
ten-hide.com

This restaurant is located on a quiet street, and is just a seven-minute walk from busy Shinnku Station. They source the best seasonal ingredients from Tsukiji Market every day for their traditional Edo-style dishes. In the evening, they only serve set menus, so go at lunch time if you just want to sample their tempura.

27   YAMANOUE

AT: HILLTOP HOTEL
1-1 Kanda Surugadai
Chiyoda-ku ⑨
+81 (0)3-3293-2831
yamanoue-hotel.co.jp/
restaurant/tenpura/

A posh restaurant in the Hilltop Hotel (in Japanese, *Yamanoue Hotel*) where many famous literary figures, such as Yukio Mishima and Yasunari Kawabata, stayed to write their novels. Don't miss their *Maruju*, a tempura of thick-cut sweet potato. We recommend sharing though because this is a big dish.

28   TENSAKU

3-2-16 Shimo-Ochiai
Shinjuku-ku ⑪
+81 (0)3-3954-1036

A popular tempura restaurant near Mejiro Station. They also serve unusual tempura, in addition to shrimp and vegetable. This depends on the seasons, of course, when sea urchin, crab, fig, *mochi* (rice cake) and baby corn are available. The friendly atmosphere makes you feel very welcome.

29 MIYAKAWA

6-1-6 Minami-Aoyama
Minato-ku ④
+81 (0)3-3400-3722

A small Kansai-style tempura restaurant on the opposite side of the Nezu Museum. In Kanto, an egg is added to the batter whereas they don't usually do this in Kansai. The prawns, scallop, aubergine, and other seasonal ingredients in the thin batter are very crispy. Like so many other tempura restaurants, the lunch is very reasonable in price.

30 TSUNAHACHI

3-31-8 Shinjuku
Shinjuku-ku ⑦
+81 (0)3-3352-1012
tunahachi.co.jp/en

Shinjuku is a hotspot for fashion lovers, and fans of tempura. This restaurant has been serving good quality tempura at reasonable prices for almost 100 years. Take a seat at the counter to see how the ingredients are delicately fried in refreshing rice oil and try the ice cream tempura while you're at it.

27 YAMANOUE

31 KANDA MATSUYA

The 5 best places for
JAPANESE NOODLES

---

31 KANDA MATSUYA
1-13 Kanda-Sudacho
Chiyoda-ku ⑨
+81 (0)3-3251-1556
kanda-matsuya.jp

They have been serving hand-kneaded *soba* (buckwheat noodle) here since the Meiji period. *Goma* (sesame) *soba* is the owner's recommended menu and also the most popular one for women. The *Sobagaki* (a dumpling made of buckwheat and water) and *Ten-Nanban* (tempura soba) are also very good.

32 SARASHINA HORII
3-11-4 Moto-Azabu
Minato-ku ⑥
+81 (0)3-3403-3401
sarashina-horii.com

This restaurant is said to have opened over 200 years ago. Their signature menu of *Sarashina Soba* consists of white noodles that are made of buckwheat kernels. The seasonal *soba* is prepared with *Sarashina Soba* mixed with an ingredient. You can also choose between two types of dipping sauces.

33 MATSUO
2-1-7 Sarugaku-cho
Chiyoda-ku ⑨
+81 (0)3-3291-3529

The menu has plenty of options but if you can't decide then order *Nishoku-mori*, or two different flavours on one plate. They also have a variety of side dishes, including tempura and *yaki-miso* (grilled miso). Try *sobagaki* with red bean paste if you still have some room for dessert.

34 KYOURAKUTEI

3-6 Kagurazaka
Shinjuku-ku ⑤
+81 (0)3-3269-3233
kyourakutei.com

Located off Kagurazaka. The noodles here are made of stone-ground buckwheat and are very popular with *soba* fanatics. Their *Zaru Soba* are prepared with 100% buckwheat, without wheat flour, making them a good option for anyone on a gluten-free diet. They also serve a wide selection of sakes. Have some with a stewed beef tendon.

35 SATAKE

AT: DAIKOKU BUILDING
1-8-14 Ebisu
Shibuya-ku ②
+82 (0)3-5877-2698
satake-ebisu-
sobanoodle-shop.
business.site

Satake calls itself a 'fast-food' shop. Place your order at the machine at the entrance, then hand it to the people behind the counter, take a seat, and a bowl of piping hot *soba* will appear on your table within minutes. They serve 100% buckwheat noodles here, and the soup is made without additives. The place to go for top quality *soba* at a good price!

5 *great places for*
RAMEN

---

36 **TENHO**
7-8-5 Roppongi
Minato-ku ⑥
+81 (0)3-3404-6155

Located in a building in front of Tokyo Midtown. The noodles of their '1-3-5 Ramen' are chewier, and their soy sauce-based soup is oilier and saltier. *Menbari* is an alternative version of their 1-3-5 Ramen with an even tougher noodle. Once you taste it, you might find it highly addictive however.

37 **MENYA ISHIN**
3-4-1 Kami-Osaki
Meguro-ku ②
+81 (0)3-3444-8480

If you are not that keen on oily and fatty foods but want to eat ramen, then this is the place for you. Their soup is clear in colour but has a good texture, and you will find that you simply cannot resist having it all. Don't forget to sample their *wonton* (Chinese dumpling)!

38 **MENYA NUKAJI**
3-12 Udagawacho
Shibuya-ku ①
+81 (0)90-3801-8247

They serve both ramen and tukemen (dipping noodles). Their soup is a mixture of meat broth and fish broth – thick but not too heavy. If you are in Tokyo in the summer, then try their *Katsuo-dashi no Hiyashi Niku Soba* (meat noodles in a cold bonito soup).

39 **RAMEN JIRO**

**2-16-4 Mita
Minato-ku** ⑥

Ramen Jiro is a cult restaurant among ramen lovers. Memorise a few Japanese words before going so you can customise your order, such as *nin-niku* (garlic), *yasai* (vegetable), and *karame* (thicker soup), *abura* (oil), and *sono mama* (without topping). Their portions tend to be substantial, so you can order a smaller portion if you wish.

40 **AOBA**

**5-58-1 Nakano
Nakano-ku** ⑫
+81 (0)3-3388-5552
nakano-aoba.jp

They use 'double soup' at Aoba, made from chicken and pork bones combined with seafood stock. It's very easy to digest, which may well be one of the reasons why this place is so popular. Aoba has 20 ramen shops in and outside Tokyo.

The 5 best places for
ONIGIRI
(rice balls)

---

41 OMUSUBI CAFE

3-7 Sarugakucho
Shibuya-ku ①
+81 (0)3-6321-0168
omusubi-cafe.jp

Here at Omosubi Café, they prepare *omusubi* (another name for *onigiri)* from morning till evening with additive-free ingredients only. The side dishes, which are served with a rice ball as a set meal, including marinated fried chicken, are equally delicious. You have a choice of brown or white rice. The menu also includes Japanese sweets if you still have some room for dessert.

42 OHITSUZEN TANBO

1-41-9 Yoyogi
Shibuya-ku ⑦
+81 (0)3-3320-0727
tanbo.co.jp

Ohitsu is a wooden container for cooked rice, which controls moisture. Here they serve a set menu with rice in such a container as well as selling bento boxes and rice balls. They make rice balls to order so you can always enjoy fresh ones.

43 ONIGIRI BONGO

2-27-5 Kita-Otsuka
Toshima-ku ⑪
+81 (0)3-3910-5617
onigiribongo.info

Here you can sit at the counter, like in a sushi shop, and order what you like. They then prepare it for you and you can eat fresh *onigiri*, that is still warm. Choose from over 50 toppings. Pay an additional 50 yen to have two toppings on a piece of *onigiri*.

44 ONIGIRI ASAKUSA YADOROKU

3-9-10 Asakusa Taito-ku ⑩
+81 (0)3-3874-1615
onigiriyadoroku.com

This is the oldest *onigiri* shop in Tokyo. They source their rice and ingredients from all over Japan. You can eat your *onigiri* inside the shop with a bowl of tasty miso soup or take out your meal. You can order by the piece, so why not have some *onigiri* as a snack? Simple but satisfying.

45 ONIGIRIYA MARUTOYO

4-9-9 Tsukiji Chuo-ku ⑧
+81 (0)3-3541-6010

A reputable shop in Tsukiji Market. They have a great selection – from traditional *onigiri*, such as salmon and pickled plums, to more unusual options, such as *ebi-furai* (deep fried prawn). Do try their *Oyako* (meaning parent and child, in this case, salmon and salmon roe).

44 ONIGIRI ASAKUSA YADOROKU

5 great
GYOZA RESTAURANTS

46 **GYOZA NO FUKUHO**
2-8-6 Shinjuku
Shinjuku-ku ⑦
+81 (0)3-5367-1582
fukuho.net

People are always queueing here. They have two types of *gyoza*, *yaki gyoza* (grilled) and *sui gyoza* (boiled), both of which contain plenty of vegetables, making this a healthy option. The former is crispy, while the latter one has a *mochi*-like texture – soft and squishy.

47 **HARAJUKU GYOZARO**
6-2-4 Jingumae
Shibuya-ku ③
+81 (0)3-3406-4743

Despite its location, this place is not that expensive, which is why it is always crowded. They serve two types of *gyoza*: *yaki gyoza* and *sui gyoza*, with or without *nin-niku* (garlic) and *nira* (Chinese chive). Try the crispy grilled *gyoza*, which contain a lot of meat juice.

48 **FUJIIYA**
2-21-11 Misakicho
Chiyoda-ku ⑨
+81 (0)3-3239-8295

In addition to traditional *gyoza* (which they call *Ganso Gyoza*), they also serve *Ebi Nira* (prawn and Chinese chive) *Gyoza*, *Pari Pari* (crispy) *Gyoza*, *Shiso* (Japanese basil) *Gyoza*, and much more. Make life easy and just order *Zenpin Moriawase* – four different types of grilled *gyoza* on the same plate.

49 KAMEIDO GYOZA HONTEN

5-3-3 Kameido
Koto-ku ⑮
+81 (0)3-3681-8854
kameido-gyouza.co.jp

Their menu is as straightforward as it gets because they only serve *gyoza* here. As soon as you order a drink, the freshly-grilled *gyoza* is brought to your table. There are five pieces to a plate, and you have to eat at least ten. But don't worry; their *gyoza* are not that filling. You will find that you can easily gobble up that second plate, and order more.

50 GINZA TENRYU

AT: PUZZLE GINZA, 4TH FL.
2-15-19 Ginza
Chuo-ku ⑧
+81 (0)3-3561-3543
ginza-tenryu.com

Their *gyoza*, which are made according to their own recipe since the 1940s, are huge. Don't worry about garlic breath after eating here because the dishes don't contain any flavouring ingredients. In addition to *gyoza*, they serve authentic Pekinese cuisine.

49 KAMEIDO GYOZA HONTEN

The 5 best places to eat
JAPANESE-STYLE CURRY

---

51 **RICE CURRY MANTEN**
1-54 Kanda-Jinbocho
Chiyoda-ku ⑨
+81 (0)3-3291-3274

There are more than 30 curry shops in Jinbocho. Manten is one of the more affordable ones in the area. *Katsu* (deep-fried pork cutlet) and *korokke* (croquette) are the two most popular toppings. If you are super-hungry, order a *Zenbu-Nose* (an everything curry) – you can have *katsu*, *korroke*, sausage and *gyoza* all in one go!

52 **KYOEIDO**
AT: SAN BUILDING, B1
1-6 Kanda-Jinbocho
Chiyoda-ku ⑨
+81 (0)3-3291-1475
kyoueidoo.com

This restaurant opened in 1924. The chef introduced Sumatran-style curry to Japan (but he tweaked the recipe a bit so the Japanese would really love it). From October until April, they serve baked apples with a dollop of fresh cream. Don't miss out as they only prepare 25-30 portions a day.

53 **GRILL SWISS**
AT: OKURA ANNEX, 2ND FL.
3-4-4 Ginza
Chuo-ku ⑧
+81 (0)3-3563-3206
ginza-swiss.com

This was the first shop to serve katsu curry. Their curry sauce, which tastes delicious with the cutlet, is made using various vegetables and fruit, including onion, carrot, and apple. You can order a *hire-katsu* (deep-fried pork fillet) curry sandwich and curry rice to take away.

54 MATSUMOTORO

AT: HIBIYA PARK
1-2 Hibiya Koen
Chiyoda-ku ⑧
+81 (0)3-3503-1451
matsumotoro.co.jp

When Hibiya Park, the first Western-style park in Japan, opened in 1903, this restaurant opened at the same time, in the park. As it was very sophisticated and stylish, many artists and authors, including Soseki Natsume, loved eating curry rice and having a coffee here. Enjoy your curry and the lovely view!

55 KITCHEN NANKAI

**1-39-8 Kanda-
Jinbocho
Chiyoda-ku** ⑨
+81 (0)3-3219-1616

Another shop in Jinbocho. Their most popular dish is *katsu* curry, but their just-fried cutlet comes in a darkish curry, verging on black. Around lunch, there is always a queue of *sarari man* (office workers) who need an energy boost for the afternoon.

55 KITCHEN NANKAI

5 must-visit restaurants for
MEAT LOVERS

---

56 **TORI CHATARO**
7-12 Uguisudanicho
Shibuya-ku ①
+81 (0)3-6416-0364

As this place is far from the centre of Shibuya, this *yakitori* restaurant is a real hidden gem. *Yakitori* places tend to be noisy, but this one is a little more sophisticated. Enjoy excellent chicken while listening to hits from the last century (probably the chef's favourite genre).

57 **REBAYA**
AT: KR BUILDING
1-22-12 Yotsuya
Shinjuku-ku ⑤
+81 (0)3-6380-4988

There are several good *izakaya* on Shinmichi-dori in Yotsuya. This *yakitori* place serves some special options, including *chochin* (egg), *saezuri* (throat), and *shiro reba* (white liver). Limited availability, so I recommend going there early in the evening.

58 **HAGAKURE**
2-8-11 Shibuya
Shibuya-ku ①
+81 (0)3-3400-3294

Located on the upper floor of an old building between Shibuya and Omotesando. This place serves *Yakiton* (grilled pork). Don't worry if you don't know what to order – just say *omakase* (which means 'you decide for me'). Be careful not to drink too much, or you might fall down the stairs on the way out.

59 SANBYAKUYA

12-4 Shinsencho
Shibuya-ku ①
+81 (0)3-3477-1129
sanbyakuya.com

Shinsen is located within walking distance from Shibuya and is one of the up and coming areas where there are many excellent restaurants. At Sanbyakuya, they start by serving you a pile of shredded cabbage, which you should eat in between meat dishes to promote good digestion.

60 SHINJUKU HORUMON

3-12-3 Shinjuku
Shinjuku-ku ⑦
+81 (0)3-3353-4129

Horumon-yaki, grilled beef and pork offal, is an excellent way to consume mineral and collagen and the Japanese love it. They also serve other cuts you might be more familiar with, such as tripe or skirt steak. Their retro-style interiors will make you feel as if you have travelled back in time to the Showa period.

60 SHINJUKU HORUMON

The 5 best shops for
SHAVED ICE

---

61 TORAYA

4-9-22 Akasaka
Minato-ku ⑤
+81 (0)3-3408-2331
*global.toraya-
group.co.jp*

Toraya is one of the oldest Japanese confectionery shops and is said to have opened in the late Muromachi era (in the 16th century!). They usually start serving shaved ice from late spring until September. Their original ginger syrups can work miracles, energising any tired body.

62 SANTOKUDO

7-8-19 Ginza
Chuo-ku ⑧
+81 (0)3-3289-3131
santokudo.jp

This black tea speciality shop serves Taiwanese-style shaved ice in summer. Do try the one with Taiwan's best quality apple mango. You may be surprised at first as the ice is literally covered in mango chunks but they cut up a whole mango for each serving!

63 NANIWAYA

2-12-4 Asakusa
Taito-ku 10
+81 (0)3-3842-0988
a-naniwaya.com

This is actually a *tai-yaki* (fish-shaped cake) shop but they also serve shaved ice in summer. *Asayake* (meaning 'dawn'), which comes with toppings of red bean paste, milk, and strawberry sauce, is the most delightful flavour combo. The homemade seasonal fruit syrups are equally delicious.

65 BLUE BRICK LOUNGE

64 RYAN

**7 Arakicho
Shinjuku-ku ⑦**

A bar off the street that only serves shaved ice in the afternoon in summer and autumn. Their syrups, which are made with seasonal fruit, are delicious when used as a topping on the airy, soft pieces of ice. You can order *aigake* (half and half) for a taste of two types of syrup. Check their Twitter for more information.

65 BLUE BRICK LOUNGE

**5-3-3 Minami-
Aoyama
Minato-ku ④
+81 (0)3-5485-3340
*yokumoku.co.jp/en***

This cafe in popular confectionary shop Yoku Moku serves shaved ice from late June until mid-September, using natural ice cream made by artisans in Nikko. The menu also features some light snacks, like a *galette* (buckwheat pancake) or a croque-monsieur.

65 BLUE BRICK LOUNGE

5 superb
ICE-CREAM
parlours

---

66 **FLOTO**
4-12-6 Yoyogi
Shibuya-ku ⑦
+81 (0)3-6300-9099

Here they source fresh seasonal ingredients directly from rigorously vetted farmers across Japan. A place to enjoy flavours that you probably won't find outside Japan such as *sencha* (a type of green tea) with lemongrass and *Benihoppe* (a brand name for a premium strawberry).

67 **JAPANESE ICE OUCA**
1-6-7 Ebisu
Shibuya-ku ②
+81 (0)3-5449-0037
ice-ouca.com

Their ice cream is milky and rich but not cloyingly sweet. Three flavours of your choice are served in a cup with a rice wafer and *shio kombu* (salted kelp). The delicate sweetness of the ice cream and the saltiness of kelp will set your taste buds spinning.

68 **PREMIUM SOW**
AT: SYMPHONY
DAIKANYAMA 103
12-16 Daikanyamacho
Shibuya-ku ①
+81 (0)3-5422-3390
premium-sow.com

All of their products are vegan and gluten-free. In addition to their amazing range of ice creams, they also serve ice-cream sandwiches made with gluten-free biscuits (of course). There is a tiny counter where you can enjoy ice cream and a nice cup of coffee.

69 COCONUT GLEN'S

2-4-2 Azabu Juban
Minato-ku ⑥
+81 (0)3-6826-9266
coconutglens.jp

As you can tell by this shop's name, all their ice cream is made from coconut milk, without white sugar or eggs. The place to go for a vegan and 'guilt-free' treat. Looking for something unusual? Try their 'ginger lemongrass'! You won't regret it.

70 MITSUBACHI

3-38-10 Yushima
Bunkyo-ku ⑩
+81 (0)3-3831-3083
mitsubachi-co.com

This 100-year-old shop in Yushima serves a Japanese-style ice cream called *Ogura aisu*, which is made of red bean paste. If you are more adventurous, then order some *Ogura aisu* like the locals – such as *Ogura anmitsu* (agar jelly topped with ice cream and syrup) or *Ogura shiratama* (mochi balls topped with ice cream).

The 5 best
BAKERIES

71 **VIRON**
    33-8 Udagawa-cho
    Shibuya-ku ①
    +81 (0)3-5458-1770

Their baguette, made with proper French flour, is considered unrivalled in Japan. They have a dining room above the bakery which opens at 9 am. As Viron is located near Tokyu Department's flagship store, it is the perfect place for breakfast before you go shopping or to the cinema or a museum.

72 **365 NICHI**
    1-2-8 Tomigaya
    Shibuya-ku ⑫
    +81 (0)3-6804-7357

The owner and chef's policy is to bake bread without food additives, only using flour that is produced in Japan. As the shop's name, which means 365 days, suggests, you can buy fresh bread here every day. There is an eat-in space where you can sample of the bread straight from the oven, with a good cup of coffee.

73 **BREAD, ESPRESSO &**
    3-4-9 Jingumae
    Shibuya-ku ③
    +81 (0)3-5410-2040
    bread-espresso.jp

The owner wanted to create an Italian-style bar where people drop in every day. They open at 8 am and by lunchtime and on weekends the place is packed. Their *pain perdu* made with their signature 'Mou' (French for soft) bread is too good for words.

74 **SORA TO MUGI TO**
2-10-7 Ebisu-Nishi
Shibuya-ku ②
+81 (0)3-6427-0158
soratomugito.com

The owner grows his own organic wheat in Yamanashi to mill his own flour. Then he rigorously selects only the best ingredients for his delicious bread. Try his *Kuromame Pan*, the locals' favourite bread, with sweet black beans and pumpkin.

75 **SHIGEKUNIYA 55 BAKERY**
3-22-9 Koenji-Kita
Suginami-ku ⑫
+81 (0)3-5356-7617

This bakery originally opened in Kichijoji, became a popular fixture at the UNU Farmer's Market, and moved to the current location in 2014. They take their bread very seriously here as you can tell from the display. Try their tasty savoury and sweet bagels for something really good.

75 SHIGEKUNIYA 55 BAKERY

5
JAPANESE SNACKS
you should try

76 **KREPU**

Although it was inspired by a French pancake *crêpe*, *krepu* was originally created in Harajuku, Japan in the 1970s and has since become a typical sweet of the area. *Krepu* is a piece of pancake folded into four and topped with whipped cream and fruit, or even some chocolate sauce.

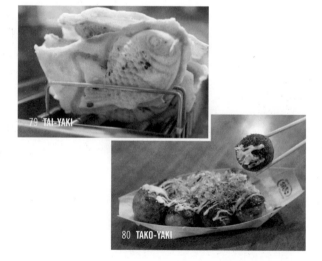

79 TAI-YAKI

80 TAKO-YAKI

77 **YAKIIMO**

Sweet potatoes baked in a stone oven. From late autumn onwards, you'll often come across food trucks which serve them. Many locals cannot resist the lure of the drivers' call, especially on a cold day. The cooks will often give you a tiny piece to taste, so why not try it?

78 **IMAGAWA-YAKI**

A small thick pancake filled with *an* (red bean paste). Sometimes also called *kaiten yaki* or *oban-yaki* depending on the region. These days you can take your pick from a wide range of fillings, including custard cream, chocolate cream, cheese cream, and so on. Eat while warm.

79 **TAI-YAKI**

Very similar in taste to *imagawa-yaki*, but *tai-yaki* is baked in a fish-shaped mould, is crispier than *imagawa-yaki* and contains more bean paste. Some of the shops sell *hane tsuki tai-yaki*, with a crispy coating.

80 **TAKO-YAKI**

Tako (octopus) + *yaki* (grill). Octopus mixed in a batter, made with flour, eggs and milk, served with pickled ginger and spring onion. Usually they will serve you six or eight balls on a plate with mayonnaise and *ao nori* (seaweed). Be careful not to burn your tongue.

5 places to eat
EGG DISHES

---

81 **KISABURO NOJO**
    1-23-11 Sengoku
    Bunkyo-ku ⑩
    +81 (0)3-3943-3746
    kisaburou-sengoku.com

Japanese people love *tamago kake ghan* (cooked rice with a raw egg). Don't be deterred by the egg however. Here they only use the freshest, best-quality eggs from a trusted source. Add a dash of soy sauce, which is specially produced for them, and you will understand why Japanese people always come back here.

82 **KISSA YOU**
    4-13-17 Ginza
    Chuo-ku ⑧
    +81 (0)3-6226-0482

A nice old *kissaten* (cafe) near Kabuki-za Theatre, which is famous for its *omuraisu*. The word *omuraisu* comes from 'omelette' with 'rice', or flavoured rice wrapped in or topped with an omelette. Although they have other dishes on the menu, most of the customers tend to order the special.

83 **KYO NO CHISO HANNARIYA**
    AT: UNO BUILDING, 2ND FL.
    1-11-15 Nihonbashi
    Muromachi
    Chuo-ku ⑧
    +81 (0)3-3245-1233
    hannariya.jp

While the Tokyo-style Japanese omelette contains sugar, its Kyoto sibling is called *dashi-maki* and is made without sugar. This restaurant serves Kyoto cuisine, and most of the lunch menu comes with a piece of *dashi-maki*, which has a delicate and fluffy texture.

84 YAKITORI MOE
3-8-12 Roppongi
Minato-ku ⑥
+81 (0)3-5414-1141

Many Japanese people eat rice dishes at the end of their meal at an *izakaya*. At this *yakitori* restaurant, customers usually order *oyako-don* (which literally translates as 'parent and child bowl' because it contains chicken and egg). Their *oyako-don* and chicken broth are so good that you could probably eat this every day.

85 CENTRE THE BAKERY
1-2-1 Ginza
Chuo-ku ⑧
+81 (0)3-3562-1016

This bakery specialises in *pain de mie* (a type of rectangular loaf), but they also serve sandwiches using their bread – they use different types of bread depending on the filling. Their *Omuretsu Sando* (egg omelette sandwich) is a sandwich with a just-cooked omelette that almost melts in your mouth.

85 CENTRE THE BAKERY

The 5 best places for
OKONOMIYAKI
and MONJAYAKI

---

86 **HASSHO**
AT: HARADA BUILDING,
2ND FL.
1-21-18 Kyodo
Setagaya-ku ⑬
+81 (0)50-5493-0940
ge2y400.gorp.jp

The most famous Hiroshima-style *okonomiyaki* restaurant in Tokyo. The chef trained at the restaurant of the same name in Hiroshima and was given the green light to open this restaurant in Tokyo. Choose a seat at the counter where the chef will amaze you with his marvellous *okonomiyaki*-making technique.

89 DARUMA

87 MOMIJIYA

4-2-6 Iidabashi
Chiyoda-ku ⑨
+81 (0)3-6272-9320
momijiya-okonomi.com

Another Hiroshima-style *okonomiyaki* restaurant. This place is so popular that there is almost always a queue outside. They serve *teppanyaki* and *yakisoba* (thin stir-fried noodles) or *yakiudon* (thick stir-fried noodles) as well as *okonomiyaki*.

88 HYOTAN

1-37-4 Asakusa
Taito-ku ⑩
+81 (0)3-3841-0589

Monjayaki, the soul food of *shitamachi* (downtown), is made with a more liquid batter than *okonomiyaki*. At *monjayaki* restaurants, a hot plate is incorporated into each table, and you are normally required to cook your dish yourself. If you are uncertain about how to do this, ask the staff – they are always helpful.

89 DARUMA

3-17-9 Tsukishima
Chuo-ku ⑮
+81 (0)3-3531-7626
tsukisima-daruma.
owst.jp/en

Although *monjayaki* is originally considered to be from Asakusa, Tsukishima is the place to be to enjoy this delicious concoction. Daruma is one of the most popular restaurants in the area. Their other menu, which includes seafood *teppanyaki,* is also good. The renovated building, a 70-year-old house, in which Daruma is based, is quite beautiful.

90 OKONOMIYAKI YAMAMOTO

1-9-11 Shinjuku
Shinjuku-ku ⑦
+81 (0)3-6384-1966

Although this place looks like a high-end, traditional restaurant, the prices on the menu are not heart-stopping. Sit at the counter to watch the organised chef-owner at work, as he prepares a rapid succession of orders.

The 5 best places for other
ASIAN CUISINE

---

91 ZUIEN BEKKAN
2-7-4 Shinjuku
Shinjuku-ku ⑦
+81 (0)3-3351-3511
zuienbekkan.co.jp

An authentic Chinese restaurant on Shinjuku Street. *Bekkan* means 'annex' in Japanese, but there is no main building. You must taste their sui gyoza – its chewy texture is too good for words. Their *xiaolongbao* (steamed bun) is also highly recommended.

92 SURAGAN
AT: QIZ EBISU B1
4-3-1 Ebisu
Shibuya-ku ②
+81 (0)3-5447-6588

Sometimes you just need a meal that gives you a bit of an energy boost, especially when the Japanese summer heat gets to you or after walking around the city all day. Consider having some *Dakhanmari* or Korean chicken stew in that case. Suragan's *bossam kimchi* is unbelievably yummy too!

93 ANGKOR WAT
1-38-13 Yoyogi
Shibuya-ku ⑦
+81 (0)3-3370-3019

A Cambodian restaurant, which opened in 1982. Their most popular dish is the stir-fried crab meat and vermicelli. The *kway teow*, served in a clear broth made from chicken bones, is also delicious. But the best thing on the menu must be their pumpkin cake, using real pumpkin skin, which is served with coconut ice cream.

94 GOLDEN BAGAN

8-20 Tomihisa-cho
Shinjuku-ku ⑦
+81 (0)3-6380-5752
goldenbagan.jp

The minute you set food in this cosy restaurant, owned by a couple from Shan State, Myanmar, you will forget that you are in the heart of Tokyo. Their set lunch is excellent and includes two of their specialities: *mohinga* (rice noodle soup) and chickpea fried rice.

95 THAILAND

3-12-10 Kinshi
Sumida-ku ⑮
+81 (0)3-3626-3885

The south exit of Kinshicho Station is known as 'Little Thailand' and this restaurant is the oldest one in the area. They import all their ingredients from Thailand, so they serve real Thai food. Their *Thai suki* is very popular, and even those who traditionally shy away from spicy food love it in equal measure.

94 GOLDEN BAGAN

5 places you should go for
LATIN-AMERICAN CUISINE

96 **FONDA DE LA MADRUGADA**

2-33-12 Jingumae Shibuya-ku ③
+81 (0)3-5410-6288
fonda-m.com

This restaurant opened in 1993 and soon became a place where people gather for a good time till dawn. They serve authentic Mexican cuisine and the music is performed by real *Mariachi*. As you go down the stairs to the basement, you might even forget that you are in Tokyo.

97 **GOSTOSO**

5-11-25 Roppongi Minato-ku ⑥
+81 (0)3-6434-0243
gostoso.jp

This Brazilian restaurant is famous for its delicious char-grilled *churrasco*. In spring and summer, you can eat outside on the terrace. On weekends, they also serve lunch. As the restaurant's name suggests, their food is *gostoso* or delicious!

98 **BANCHO**

2-13-9 Sangenjaya Setagaya-ku ⑬
+81 (0)3-5486-5488

This restaurant is a good option if you have a huge appetite but are travelling on a budget. They offer a two-hour *tabe-hodai* (all you can eat) service, during which you can enjoy 15 types of churrasco for under 5000 yen. You can add *nomi-hodai* (all you can drink) for less than 3000 yen.

99 BÉPOCAH

2-17-6 Jingumae
Shibuya-ku ③
+81 (0)3-6804-1377
bepocah.com

Until a few years ago, Japanese people had never really tasted Peruvian cuisine. Taking advantage of the growing popularity of international travel and cuisine, a few restaurants opened in Harajuku, but Bépocah is the most sophisticated one. The chef, who is originally from Peru, uses ingredients from both Peru and Japan for his lovely fusion food. Don't forget to order some Pisco with your food!

100 BARBACOA

4-3-2 Jingumae
Shibuya-ku ③
+81 (0)3-3796-0571
barbacoa.jp

If you are a real meat lover, then this Brazilian restaurant is the equivalent of meat heaven. Their salad bar offers an amazing array of sides, that are all worth trying. They have several branches in Tokyo including in Shibuya and Roppongi.

5 places to go for
A SATISFYING TAKEAWAY

---

101 FOOD TRUCK PARK
AT: OHARA-RYU KAIKAN
**5-7-17 Minami-
Aoyama
Minato-ku** ③

If you can't afford lunch in a restaurant but are tired of eating convenience store bento, a food truck is a great alternative. Every day, from Monday to Saturday, two trucks serve reasonably-priced (especially in this area!) and satisfying lunches here.

102 GINZA 6-CHOME SQUARE BUILDING
**6-17-1 Ginza
Chuo-ku** ⑧

On weekdays, office workers on their lunch break queue here at any of six or seven trucks that serve freshly made bento boxes. Then walk to Hamarikyu Gardens where you can enjoy your lunch with a view.

103 PARIYA
AT: MAKO KITA-AOYAMA
**3-12-14 Kita-Aoyama
Minato-ku** ③
+81 (03)-3409-8468
pariya.jp

Choose a main, salad, side dish, and rice for your bento box to go. This could well be the most stylish and filling bento box you'll find in Tokyo. Takeaways are also available from Scramble Square in Shibuya, Tokyo Midtown in Roppongi, and Atre Ebisu.

104 NATURAL HOUSE

3-6-18 Kita-Aoyama
Minato-ku ③
+81 (0)3-3498-2277
naturalhouse.co.jp

Natural House opened their first shop in 1982, leading the way in organic supermarkets in Japan. They have a deli counter, with all kinds of healthy options, made from carefully chosen ingredients as well as a good selection of desserts for customers with a sweet tooth.

105 KITCHEN ORIGIN

3-15-5 Higashi
Shibuya-ku ②
+81 (0)3-3498-2238
*toshu.co.jp/kitchen_*
origin/index.html

Kitchen Origin is one of the largest bento chains, with many branches in Tokyo. Here they sell bento by weight instead of offering packed bento. All you have to do is pack your own bento and pay. Their Ebisu branch is open 24 hours on weekdays.

5 restaurants
WHEN TIRED OF JAPANESE CUISINE

---

106 PIGNON
**16-3 Kamiyamacho
Shibuya-ku ①
+81 (0)3-3468-2331**

An outstanding French bistro in Oku-Shibu (literally the 'back of Shibuya'). Where to start? Their salad with grilled squid on top, liver paté, homemade lamb sausage, … There are so many delectable things on the menu and their desserts are excellent too.

107 LILLA DALARNA
AT: DAIKAN BUILDING, 2ND FL.
**6-2-7 Roppongi
Minato-ku ⑥
+81 (0)3-3478-4690
*dalarna.jp***

They have been serving Scandinavian homemade dishes here since 1979. You can have meatballs or a creamy anchovy and aubergine gratin. This place feels like to an old friend's house. You can choose bread to go with your main dish but why not have rice? Their cream sauce pairs well with rice.

108 TA-IM
**1-29-16 Ebisu
Shibuya-ku ②
+81 (0)3-5424-2990
*ta-imebisu.com***

This is one of a handful of Israeli restaurants in Tokyo. It is located between Ebisu and Hiroo. They use neither preservatives nor frozen ingredients. Their hummus and falafel are very popular. Some of their dishes can be ordered as a takeaway. They serve pita bread sandwiches for lunchtime.

109 KADAN

AT: URBAN RESORT
DAIKANYAMA, 3RD FL.
**1-3-12 Nakameguro
Meguro-ku** ②
+81 (0)3-3719-9161
kadan.tokyo

At Kadan, they are very particular about their vegetables, which they source from farmers in Kagawa and Nagano prefectures. Try their stir-fried king prawn with seasonal vegetables. A great choice if you're hungry and looking for a healthy meal.

110 SUNGARI

AT: CHIYODA BUILDING, B1
**2-45-6 Kabukicho
Shinjuku-ku** ⑦
+81 (0)50-5872-6300
sungari.jp

This Russian restaurant is an authentic Moscow-style restaurant and has been a popular fixture on the local scene for over fifty years. They serve a wide variety of dishes and vodkas. They have another branch in Shinjuku San-chome.

The 5 best
VEGETARIAN
restaurants

---

111 8ABLISH

2nd Fl., 5-10-17
Minami-Aoyama
Minato-ku ③
+81 (0)3-6805-0597
eightablish.com

The food and drink they serve here is all vegan, containing neither refined sugar nor food additives. If you eat gluten-free or have a sensitive stomach, this place might be a good option for you. The muffins and coffee are available for takeaway.

112 NAGI SHOKUDO

112 NAGI SHOKUDO

15-10 Uguisudanicho
Shibuya-ku ①
+81 (0)3-3461-3280

In 2007, the owner Akinobu Oda, who is also a writer, opened this cafe, serving vegan cuisine that pairs well with alcoholic beverages. The lunches here are very filling and taste great.

113 THREE REVIVE KITCHEN HIBIYA

AT: MIDTOWN HIBIYA,
2ND FL.
1-1-2 Yurakucho
Chiyoda-ku ⑧
+81 (0)3-6831-4620
threecosmetics.com/
shop/revive-kitchen/
hibiya

The restaurant of Japanese cosmetic brand THREE. Their concept is 'modern *shojin*' (*shojin* being traditional Buddhist cuisine), which focusses on the production and consumption of local food. If you believe that food can boost your beauty and health, then this is just the place for you.

114 BROWN RICE

BY NEAL'S YARD REMEDIES
5-1-8 Jingumae
Shibuya-ku ③
+81 (0)3-5778-5416
nealsyard.co.jp

An organic vegetarian restaurant run by UK-based Neal's Yard Remedies. Their set lunch consists of one soup and three different dishes, including pickles. They also have vegetable and bean curry. Their desserts, which are all tofu-based, such as cheesecake and ice cream, are delicious.

115 CITRON

2-27-21 Minami-
Aoyama
Minato-ku ④
+81 (0)3-6447-2556
citron.co.jp

A 'fast casual restaurant' serving healthy vegetarian cuisine. Their menu changes monthly, with a salad of the month, soup, quiche, or a sandwich. You can also customise your salad choosing the toppings and dressing you like. Their cakes are too good to resist. Vegan options available.

5 nice restaurants
WITH A VIEW

---

116 TWO ROOMS GRILL / BAR

AT: AO BUILDING, 5TH FL.
3-11-7 Kita-Aoyama
Minato-ku ③
+81 (0)3-3498-0002
tworooms.jp

This restaurant is located on the fifth floor of a landmark tower in Omotesando. From their terrace, you can enjoy a typical view of Tokyo's cityscape – lots of skyscrapers, but it all feels amazingly open and relaxing. This place doesn't just have a good view, they also serve excellent food. A kids menu is available for the under-12 crowd.

117 HANA CHIBO

AT: EBISU GARDEN PLACE TOWER, 38TH FL.
4-20-3 Ebisu
Shibuya-ku ②
+81 (0)3-5424-1011
chibo.com

This place is run by Osaka's *okonomiyaki* chain. Here, you don't have to cook your own *okonomiyaki* – their chefs make it for you. There are two counters (and tables), one where you can take in the view and another where you can enjoy the spectacle of the chef's cooking techniques.

118 MOCHIZUKI

AT: ASAHI GOUP HQ BUILDING, 21ST FL.
1-23-11 Azumabashi
Sumida-ku ⑮
+81 (0)3-5608-5002

A Japanese restaurant located on the 21st floor of the Asahi Beer Company's headquarters which is probably famous for the golden object designed by Philip Stark. From the restaurant, you can enjoy a panoramic view of the Tokyo Skytree and the Sumida River.

119 STELLAR GARDEN

AT: THE PRINCE PARK
TOWER TOKYO, 33RD FL.
**4-8-1 Shibakoen
Minato-ku** ⑥
+81 (0)3-5400-1170
princehotels.com

The bar lounge in the Prince Park Tower
Tokyo, a hotel located near the Tokyo
Tower. Their signature menu is their Kobe
beef hamburger. A bit expensive overall
because of the location, but if you want to
spend a romantic evening with the love of
your life, this can be a great choice.

120 VIEW AND DINING THE SKY

AT: HOTEL NEW OTANI,
17TH FL.
**4-1 Kioicho
Chiyoda-ku** ⑤
+81 (0)3-3238-0028
newotani.co.jp

This buffet-style restaurant slowly rotates
360 degrees. Try Japanese, Western or
Chinese food, *teppanyaki*, and sushi as well
as the desserts. The sushi here is still made
to order. They serve top-class Japanese beef
steak in the *teppanyaki* corner.

119 STELLAR GARDEN

APÉRO. WINE BAR AOYAMA

55 PLACES FOR A DRINK

5 Japanese **ALCOHOLIC BEVERAGES** ———— 86

5 **ESSENTIAL BEVERAGES**
that you can buy in a convenience store ————— 88

The 5 best places for sake ———————— 90

5 *must-visit* **BARS IN SHINJUKU
GOLDEN-GAI** ———————————— 92

The 5 best places for **JAPANESE
CRAFT BEER** ————————————— 94

5 *great* **WINE BARS** ———————— 96

The 5 best places for **JAPANESE TEA** ——— 98

The 5 cosiest **COFFEE SHOPS** ———— 100

5 **SHOWA-STYLE CAFES** ————— 102

5 **JAPANESE COCKTAILS** *you should try* —— 104

5 *great places for* **JUICES** *and* **SMOOTHIES** — 106

5 Japanese
ALCOHOLIC BEVERAGES

—————

121 **SAKE**

Sake, or Japanese rice wine, is made by fermenting rice. There are eight varieties of special designation sake, distinguished by the degree to which the rice has been polished and the percentage of malt, and whether brewing alcohol is added or not. *Junmai Daiginjo* is the highest quality. If you like sake, try the milky-coloured *Nigori-zake*, which is produced by straining sake through rough gauze.

122 **CHUHAI**

An abbreviation for '*shochu* highball'. Ordinarily a mix of *shochu*, soda, and fruit juice, mainly citrus. It is also called '*sour*' because of its taste. At some *izakaya* (Japanese-style pubs), *chuhai* is served with half a lemon or grapefruit on a press.

123 **UMESHU**

Widely known as 'plum wine'. In Japan, many people produce their own *umeshu* at home. It is not difficult to make: just steep green plums in a distilled alcoholic beverage, such as *shochu*, brandy, or white liquor. Drink it like you would drink *shochu*, or mixed with beer.

124 **AWAMORI**

This distilled alcoholic beverage is made of rice produced in Okinawa Prefecture. *Awamori* uses Indica rice (long grain) while *shochu* uses Japonica rice (short grain). The type of mould used is also different. Like *shochu*, you can drink it on the rocks, diluted with water, hot water, or soda. Add a dash of *shekwasha* (flat lemon), if you like your *awamori* old school.

125 **SHOCHU**

Distilled liquor made from wheat, buckwheat, rice, or sweet potatoes. *Kokuto* (unpurified sugar) *shochu* is produced on Amami Island and Okinawa, where sugar cane grows. If you are lucky, you may also come across other varieties of *shochu*, including chestnut, sweet corn, milk, and pumpkin.

121 SAKE

5

ESSENTIAL BEVERAGES

that you can buy in a convenience store

—————

126 COFFEE

When coffee lovers travel to Japan, they are always told to go to the nearest convenience store and try the coffee there. At first, they think it's a joke, until they take their first sip. Where else can you find good quality coffee for 100 yen (plus tax)? Unless your priority is a sofa to relax rather than taste, pop into the next convenience store for your daily dose of caffeine.

127 MITSUYA SAIDA

This carbonated drink was developed in 1884 using Japanese mineral water. It owes its flavour to fresh fruit harvested in the past 24 hours. These products do not contain preservatives. Some drinks are available in a low-calorie version.

128 POCARI SWEAT

A healthy drink that helps your body absorb water quickly, making it an ideal sports drink. Many Japanese people drink it when they have a fever, and doctors often recommend it for this purpose. It is also a good drink for a summer hike or if you had too much alcohol.

129 **AYATAKA**

A type of Japanese green tea, packaged in PET bottles and developed in collaboration with a tea shop in Uji (where *Uji-cha* is produced) that has been in business for over 450 years. It tastes so good that you might not even notice the difference with tea brewed in a teapot. From mild to full-bodied, there is one for everyone. Hot tea is also available.

130 **CALPIS**

A lactobacillus beverage that has been a favourite with Japanese people for over a century. Originally a concentrated beverage to be diluted with water, it was inspired by a drink from Inner Mongolia. Nowadays it is also sold in PET bottles. Choose from fruit-flavoured, carbonated, low-calorie and several other options.

The 5 best places for
SAKE

---

131 **FUKUBE**
1-4-5 Yaesu
Chuo-ku ⑧
+81 (0)3-3271-6065

While this *izakaya* (Japanese-style pub) has been in business for over 80 years, their selection of sake hasn't changed much since the early days. In Japan, people eat while they drink so bar food is just as important as quality of the drinks you are served. The owner of this bar goes to Tsukiji market every day to buy the catch of the day.

131 FUKUBE

132 HASEGAWA

1-18-12 Kameido
Koto-ku ⑮
+81 (0)3-5875-0404
www.hasegawa
saketen.com

The owners of this liquor shop are considered fine connoisseurs of the sake industry and have the best selection of sake in Tokyo. They also serve sake in a shot glass at the counter as well as snacks that pair very nicely with your drink. If you want to taste a line-up of different brands, then this is the place to go.

133 KAWAGUCHI

2-9-6 Nihonbashi
Chuo-ku ⑧
+81 (0)3-6225-2850

A standing sake bar. The manager used to be a sushi chef, so he has his own policy when it comes to fish – he does not use farmed fish and thinks about how best to serve fish so that it pairs nicely with your drink.

134 KURI

AT: TONY BUILDING,
2ND FL.
6-4-15 Ginza
Chuo-ku ⑧
+81 (0)3-3573-8033

A small bar in Ginza that serves 50 to 100 brands of sake and 20 brands of *shochu*. If you can't find a brand you like here, you won't find it anywhere else. When the bar is busy, they may not be able to take phone enquiries, so make sure you have Google Maps on your phone.

135 UTOU

AT: KONISHIS BUILDING,
2ND FL.
3-31-10 Nishiogi-Kita
Suginami-ku
+81 (0)3-3399-1890

Nishi-Ogikubo, often called 'Nishi Ogi', is very popular with intellectuals and antiques lovers. As this shop is said to serve the best warm sake in all of Japan, you can usually find loads of sake enthusiasts here. The *oden* they serve, with a ginger and miso paste, is simply excellent.

5 must-visit
BARS IN SHINJUKU GOLDEN-GAI

---

136 AKABANA
1-1-8 Kabukicho
Shinjuku-ku ⑦

This bar serves a good selection of *awamori* (Okinawa's *shochu*) and Okinawan cuisine. You can drink *awamori* diluted with turmeric tea or *sanpin-cha* (jasmine tea) just like in Okinawa. It is always crowded with regulars who love the friendly owner's home cooking.

137 ISHI NO HANA
1-1-10 Kabukicho
Shinjuku-ku ⑦
+81 (0)3-3200-8458

A small Russian *izakaya* that opened in 1973, making it one of the oldest in the area. The owner will gladly get out his guitar when asked. Do try their selection of vodkas if you go – some of them are quite rare.

138 BAR 5GALLON
1-1-8 Shinjuku
Shinjuku-ku ⑦
+81 (0)70-6985-7055

This friendly ambience in this bar will immediately make you feel at ease. They became famous for their curry after a popular TV presenter gave it a rave review. Homemade *otoshi* (a small dish served as a cover charge) changes daily and is much more than a small dish. Here you definitely won't leave hungry.

139 BAR URAMEN

**1-1-7 Kabukicho
Shinjuku-ku** ⑦
+81 (0)80-4369-9713

A themed *otaku* bar: home electrical appliances and digital gadgets as well as retro games. Enjoy drinks and games here, as they have roughly 600 FamiCon cassettes, while listening to some weirdly cool music.

140 TACHIBANA SHINSATSUSHITSU

**1-1-8 Kabukicho
Shinjuku-ku** ⑦
+81 (0)3-3208-4148

This bar's concept is that of a waiting room at a hospital. The staff wear nurse uniforms. All the cocktails have unique names. If you do not understand Japanese, ask the *nurse*. But be warned, some of the names are rather outrageous. Don't be disgusted, it is just their unique sense of humour.

GOLDEN-GAI

140 TACHIBANA SHINSATSUSHITSU

The 5 best places for
JAPANESE CRAFT BEER

141 T.Y. HARBOR

2-1-3 Higashi-
Shinagawa
Shinagawa-ku ⑭
+81 (0)3-5479-4555
tysons.jp

This place started out as brewery restaurant in 1997, three years after the ban on producing craft beers was lifted, renovating part of a warehouse. Beer is an ingredient in some of the dishes on the menu, including grilled ale-marinated chicken and mussels steamed in ale.

142 HINOMOTO BREWING & BEER STAND

5-71-3 Honkomagome
Bunkyo-ku ⑩
+81 (0)80-7470-5539

This bar has eight Japanese craft beer brands on tap. Some are even made on the premises. They only have a few snacks on the menu to go with the beers, except on (some) weekends when they organise special snack events.

143 NIHONBASHI BREWERY

AT: &WORK NIHONBASHI
10-13 Nihonbashi
Tomizawacho
Chuo-ku ⑨
+81 (0)3-6231-0226

You can enjoy 15 brands of craft beer including the original one specially created by Oregon's HUB (Hop works Urban Brewery). They use pesticide-free or low pesticide ingredients for the food menu. There is another shop near Tokyo Station.

144 SPRING VALLEY BREWERY TOKYO

AT: LOG ROAD DAIKANYAMA
13-1 Daikanyamacho
Shibuya-ku ②
+81 (0)3-6416-4960
springvalleybrewery.jp/ pub/tokyo

This beer dining bar is run by Japan's leading beer manufacturer Kirin. They serve six regular craft beers (strictly speaking, two of them are categorised as 'law-malt beers' under Japanese law) that are brewed in-house and others as 'on tap today.' The menu, which includes anything from steak to chocolate cake, has been chosen to pair with the beers.

145 CRAFT BEER MARKET

AT: SUMITOMO SHOJI JINBOCHO BUILDING
2-11-15 Kanda
Jinbocho
Chiyoda-ku ⑨
+81 (0)3-6272-5652
craftbeermarket.jp

They sell about 30 different craft beers here including Japanese and import brands. If you don't want to stop at one, then perhaps you should consider the *nomi hodai* option (drink all you can). Their signature food is roast chicken.

5 *great*
WINE BARS

---

146 **AOI**
2nd Fl.
1-18-9 Sekiguchi
Bunkyo-ku ⑩
+81 (0)3-6823-8246
winebar-aoi.com

This wine bar serves a selection of Japanese wines as well as French, Italian, Californian, and other import wines. They serve a selection of cheeses chosen by an affineur and snacks made from Japanese ingredients that go well with wines. They occasionally organise tastings.

147 **BAR À VIN PARTAGER**
AT: OMOTESANDO HILLS,
3RD FL.
4-12-10 Jingumae
Shibuya-ku ③
+81 (0)3-6434-9091
*partager-
omotesando.com*

A wine bar in Omotesando Hills that serves wine from Japan, Europe and South America, and champagne at reasonable prices. Half a glass of wine will set you back just under 300 yen! They also serve their casual take on top-notch French cuisine. Do order their foie gras macaron.

148 **3AMOURS**
1-15-9 Ebisu-Nishi
Shibuya-ku ②
+81 (0)3-5459-4333
3amours.com

A wine bar in a wine shop. You can enjoy a glass (or glasses) of organic wine at a reasonable price – even if you are on your own. A nice wine shop where you may discover some interesting and rare finds. Bear in mind they close at 9 pm.

149 NUMÉRO CINQ

4-1 Tsukudocho
Shinjuku-ku ⑤
+81 (0)3-6228-1596
kansui-office.com/
numéro-cinq

This tiny bar, which is always crowded, serves reasonably-priced wines and champagnes. There are lots of food options too, none of them disappointing. Their French fries served with sour cream are simply addictive! Once you start eating, you'll find it very hard to stop.

150 APÉRO. WINE BAR AOYAMA

3-4-6 Minami-Aoyama
Minato-ku ④
+81 (0)3-6325-3893
apero.co.jp

A wine bar run by a French couple serving organic, biodynamic, or natural wines imported from wineries that were personally selected by the owner. They serve French cuisine made with organic Japanese ingredients and organise fun-filled events.

150 APÉRO. WINE BAR AOYAMA

The 5 best places for
JAPANESE TEA

---

151 CHA CHA NO MA

5-13-14 Jingumae
Shibuya-ku ③
+81 (0)3-5468-8846
chachanoma.com

Tea sommelier Yoshi Watada serves a selection of teas from all over Japan. The food menu, including homemade sweets, is excellent and their *matcha* (green tea) ice cream comes highly recommended. Don't forget to order *kiseki no itteki* (which is a surprise drink).

152 UOGASHI MEICHA

5-5-6 Ginza
Chuo-ku ⑧
+81 (0)3-3571-1211
uogashi-meicha.co.jp

Their main shop is located right in the heart of Tsukiji Market and has been popular with people in Tokyo for many years. Their Ginza shop is the place to go for a nice cup of tea with a slice of seasonal Japanese cake. Their light-coloured *hoji-cha* (roasted tea) is very mild.

153 KOSOAN

1-24-23 Jiyugaoka
Meguro-ku ⑬
+81 (0)3-3718-4203
kosoan.co.jp

A cafe in an old traditional house that was built over a century ago. You might be forgiven for thinking that you escaped busy Tokyo as you gaze at their lovely Japanese garden. Enjoy your bowl of *matcha* in this soothing atmosphere. Their antique furniture is also worth looking at.

154 **CHA-NO-HA**
AT: MATSUYA GINZA
3-6-1 Ginza
Chuo-ku ⑧
+81 (0)3-3567-2635
chanoha.info

Located in the basement of Matsuya, behind the retail space. You can enjoy tea and seasonal sweets at the counter. This place is a real life-saver when you need a break from shopping in Ginza. The menu is seasonal.

155 **CHA CHA KOBO**
2-21-19 Nishi-Waseda
Shinjuku-ku ⑪
+81 (0)3-3203-2033
chachakoubou.com

This cafe serves organic Japanese tea and Japanese sweets, including *matcha* ice cream and *zenzai* (*mochi* and sweet red bean sauce). They also have rice balls at lunch, and *udon* noodles and bowl food in the evening.

153 **KOSOAN**

The 5 cosiest
COFFEE SHOPS

---

156 MANMANDO
3-15-4 Nishi-Nippori
Arakawa-ku ⑩
+81 (0)3-3824-4800

This cafe has a unique atmosphere, with antique furniture and the pleasing aroma of homeroasted beans. The owner does not believe in compromises when it comes to beans. Some of the beans they roast here are so rare that you should give them a try.

158 KANDA COFFEE

157 KOFFEE MAMEYA

4-15-3 Jingumae
Shibuya-ku ③
+81 (0)3-5413-9422
koffee-mameya.com

Walk up to the counter and wait for the baristas to greet you. They will then ask you about your taste preferences to find the best match for you. Standing room only.

158 KANDA COFFEE

2-38-10 Kanda
Jinbocho
Chiyoda-ku ⑨
+81 (0)3-5213-4337

A coffee house located in an area with plenty of bookshops. A pretty red roaster welcomes you when you get tired of book-hunting. Many business people like to come here for a coffee on their lunch break.

159 TORANOKO

6-14 Yotsuya Saneicho
Shinjuku-ku ⑤
+81 (0)3-6670-5532
toranokocoffee.com

When you order a cup of drip coffee, they will ask you what kind of coffee you prefer. Explain whether you prefer something more bitter, or something with more acidity, so they can make just the right choice for you. Try the crème caramel dessert that pairs nicely with your coffee.

160 JALK COFFEE

4-19-4 Eifuku
Suginami-ku ⑫
+81 (0)3-6379-1313
jalkcoffee.com

Their concept is 'to offer people a bit of happiness with coffee in their daily life'. Good news for coffee addicts: the second cup is half-price. Do try their homemade chiffon cake.

5
SHOWA-STYLE CAFES

---

161 COFFEE L'AMBRE
3-31-3 Shinjuku
Shinjuku-ku ⑦
+81 (0)3-3352-3361

A boring characterless cafe at first glance, but walk downstairs and it's like travelling back in time to the Showa period (1926-1989). As they are open till late, this is a good option for an after-dinner coffee.

162 MILONGA NUEVA
1-3-3 Kanda Jinbocho
Chiyoda-ku ⑨
+81 (0)3-3295-1716

There are several old cafes in Jinbocho, and this perhaps is one of the most famous ones. As the name suggests, this is a tango cafe where live tango concerts are sometimes held. Try their pear tart or chocolate pudding, which both taste equally well with coffee. They also serve beer.

163 LADRIO
1-3 Kanda Jinbocho
Chiyoda-ku ⑨
+81 (0)3-3295-4788

This cafe, which is located in the same alley as Milonga, resonates with French chansons. They are the first cafe to serve Wiener coffee. Wax nostalgic as you listen to the distinctive sound of vinyl records in dimmed light over a coffee.

164 MEIKYOKU KISSA LION

2-19-13 Dogenzaka
Shibuya-ku ①
+81 (0)3-3461-6858
lion.main.jp

A *meikyoku kissa* is a type of cafe where customers can enjoy classical music (often played on an expensive audio system) while enjoying coffee or tea. This cafe opened in 1926. It was burnt down during WWII but subsequently reopened. Please note that taking pictures and using a mobile phone is not allowed here.

165 CAFÉ PAULISTA

8-9-16 Ginza
Chuo-ku ⑮
+81 (0)3-3572-6160
paulista.co.jp

The term *Ginbura*, which means drinking Brazilian coffee in Ginza, was coined by the regulars of this cafe. Café Paulista opened in 1911 and is popular with a great many people including the legendary John Lennon. The coffee beans they use are certified organic.

161 COFFEE L'AMBRE

5
JAPANESE COCKTAILS
you should try

---

166 YUKIGUNI

Keiichi Iyama created the Yukiguni, which means 'snow country', in the 1950s. This cocktail is made from vodka, white curaçao, and lime cordial. Usually, the glass has a sugar rim, reminding you of a snowy winter scene. Sweet but low-proof.

170 **MIXOLOGY SALON**

167 CHERRY BLOSSOM

Many people visit Japan in late March to early April to see the *sakura* or cherry blossoms. This cocktail, which was created in the Taisho period, is made from cherry liquor, brandy, orange curaçao, lemon juice, and grenadine syrup. You can drink this cocktail outside of Japan, in which case it is usually made with gin instead of brandy.

168 SAKETINI

The Japanese version of a martini, using sake instead of vermouth. The garnish usually is *umeboshi* (pickled plum) instead of an olive – striking just the right note between the dryness of gin and the sweetness of sake.

169 SAMURAI ROCK

You might think this is a strong cocktail, but it isn't. Samurai is made of sake and lime juice. On the rocks is a popular way to drink it. If you come to Japan in spring or summer, you can buy packed or bottled Samurai at a liquor shop.

170 TEA COCKTAILS AT MIXOLOGY SALON

AT: GINZA SIX, 13TH FL.
6-10-1 Ginza
Chuo-ku ⑧
+81 3-6280-6622
ginza6.tokyo/
shops/1239

Not the name of a cocktail, but if you plan to go shopping or see Kabuki or Noh in the Ginza area, you should visit the Mixology Salon on the 13th floor of Ginza Six. They have a great selection of cocktails with tea and seasonal ingredients. Mocktails available too.

5 great places for
JUICES and SMOOTHIES

---

171 TOKYO JUICE
3-1-24 Jingumae
Shibuya-ku ④
+81 (0)3-6883-3602
tokyojuice.co.jp

At this shop, located off Gaien Nishi-Dori avenue, you feel relaxed while sipping your drink at one of the white tables out front. They have a great selection of raw juices and smoothies, so there's always something to your liking. They use homemade nut milk for the smoothies, to make it even healthier.

172 DAVID OTTO
2-6-3 Sendagaya
Shibuya-ku ③
+81 (0)3-6758-0620
davidottojuice.com

A Tokyo branch of a Californian cold-pressed juice shop. Their coconut water is sourced from old coconut, so its texture is thicker than the water of young coconuts. You can add a scoop of coconut ice cream from Kippy's Coco Cream which share this shop space with David Otto.

173 CLEANSING CAFE
AT: URBAN PARK
DAIKANYAMA II 212
9-8 Sarugakucho
Shibuya-ku ②
+81 (0)3-6277-5336
cleansingcafe.com

In addition to a variety of cold-pressed juices, including seasonal ones, they also serve soup as a detox option. They recommend having some wild rice with it. You can take away juice and soup. They can also put together a diet menu for you.

174 SUNSHINE JUICE

1-5-8 Ebisu
Shibuya-ku ②
+81 (0)3-6277-3122
sunshinejuice.jp

The pioneer of cold-pressed juice in Japan. They use locally-sourced ingredients as much as possible. They even visit farmers to see how fruit and vegetables are grown and buy ugly fruit and vegetables that won't make it to market. As you can see, their juice makes everyone happy. Smoothies and vegan soups also available.

175 SKY HIGH DAIKANYAMA

19-18 Uguisudanicho
Shibuya-ku ①
+81 (0)3-6416-0819
skyhigh-tokyo.jp

Sky High is the first juice bar to serve cold-pressed juices in Tokyo. Choosing a juice or smoothie can be hard as there are so many good choices to pick from. They also offer snacks, including kale wraps and smoothie bowls, which are real energy boosters.

KAKIMORI

100 PLACES TO SHOP

---

5 rising Japanese DESIGNERS —————— 112

5 great OUTDOOR CLOTHING shops ——— 114

5 JEWELLERY shops by young designers ——— 116

5 DESIGNER CLOTHES shops —————— 118

5 not-to-miss VINTAGE shops —————— 120

5 great places to BUY A KIMONO ————— 122

5 must-visit CONCEPT STORES————— 124

The 5 best INTERIOR DESIGN shops ——— 126

5 nice CRAFT shops —————————— 128

5 of the best DEPA-CHIKA (food halls) ——— 130

The 5 best JAPANESE SWEET shops ——— 132

The 5 best **PATISSERIES** ——————————— 134

5 essential **INTERNATIONAL FOOD** *stores* —— 136

5 **STALLS** *and* **FOOD TRUCKS** *at the*
UNU *Farmer's Market* ——————————— 138

5 **SPECIALIST SHOPS** ——————————— 141

5 interesting **CD** *and* **VINYL SHOPS** ————— 143

The 5 best **BOOKSHOPS** ——————————— 145

5 **STATIONERY** *shops to check out* ——————— 148

5 **STATIONERY ITEMS** *you should buy* ———— 150

The 5 best **100 YEN / 300 YEN SHOPS** ——— 152

5 rising Japanese
DESIGNERS

176 **MAME KUROGOUCHI**

3-8-3 Kita-Aoyama
Minato-ku ③
mamekurogouchi.com

The brand was launched in 2010 by designer Maiko Kurogouchi, who used to work at Issey Miyake. Although the fashion industry tends to go for more unisex styles, her designs are chic and feminine, and her versatile jersey dresses are tremendously popular.

178 UJOH

177 CHIKA KISADA

AT: RESTYLE,
ISETAN SHINJUKU
3-14-1 Shinjuku
Shinjuku-ku ⑦
chikakisada.com

Rekisami's designer Chika Kisada launched her own brand in 2014. Her concept is 'vital elegance', inspired by the sophistication of ballet elegance and the vitality of the punk movement. Her three-dimensional creations come to life when worn.

178 UJOH

AT: THE TOKYO,
OMOTESANDO HILLS,
2ND FL.
4-12-10 Jingumae
Shibuya-ku ③
ujoh.official.ec

UJOH was established by Mitsuru Nishizaki, who started his career working at Yohji Yamamoto and Y's as a pattern maker. Since the brand's launch in 2009, Nishizaki has gone on to create unique and often asymmetric designs for men and women. If you want to stand out from the crowd, this is the place to shop.

179 YOHEI OHNO

AT: RESTYLE,
ISETAN SHINJUKU
3-14-1 Shinjuku
Shinjuku-ku ⑦
yoheiohno.com

In 2014, Yohei Ohno, who was in his late 20s, launched his own brand. He approaches clothes like product design, so you can use your imagination to style his designs as you choose. He also works for '3711 Project', creating unique pieces using vintage kimono fabrics.

180 MASU

AT: SHELTER
2-2-5 Ebisu Nishi
Shibuya-ku ②
+81 (0)3-3464-9466

The brand name is pronounced as 'em ei es ju'. MASU's creations are inspired by *amekaji,* a popular style among Japanese teens which draws on a stereotypical of American, casual style. He combines vivid colours like red, cobalt blue, or fuchsia pink, for his elegant designs.

5 great
OUTDOOR CLOTHING
shops

---

181 AND WANDER

AT: MIYASHITA PARK SOUTH,
2ND FL.
6-20-10 Jingumae
Shibuya-ku ②
+81 (0)3-6433-5485
andwander.com

Keita Ikeuchi and Mihoko Mori, who used to work at Issey Miyake, launched this efficient, stylish outdoor clothing brand in 2011. Many overseas brands, including Maison Kitsuné and Barbour, have already turned to And Wander for collabs. Some items come in various sizes, from women's S to men's XL.

182 NANAMICA

26-13 Sarugakucho
Shibuya-ku ②
+81 (0)3-5728-6550
nanamica.com

The pioneer of 'urban outdoor' style in Japan. Eiichiro Homma and Takashi Imaki, who launched the brand, worked for sports brands for many years and were inspired to create a collection of practical clothes that could be worn in daily life. The North Face Purple Label is a collab with American brand The North Face.

183 MONT-BELL

1-8-12 Ebisu
Shibuya-ku ②
+81 (0)3-5420-7956
montbell.jp

Their products are known for being practical and reasonable. They offer a wide range of sizes, some items even come in kids' sizes. One of the best-selling products is a folding UV umbrella, which is highly effective for Japan's hot, humid summer.

184 SNOW PEAK

6-2-6 Jingumae
Shibuya-ku ③
+81 (0)3-6805-1452
snowpeak.co.jp

Tsubame-Sanjo is one of the craft centres of Japan, specialising in handmade kitchenware and tools for artisans and is where Snow Peak is based. They offer a wide range of outdoor clothing that can be worn as streetwear and equipment and organise tours and events. Their 'outdoor kimono' is unique but practical.

185 MOUNTAIN RESEARCH

AT: BEAMS PLUS HARAJUKU
3-25-12 Jingumae
Shibuya-ku ③
+81 (0)3-3746-5851

Setsumasa Kobayashi, the designer of Japanese fashion brand General Research, launched a clothing line for mountain living. The clothes he creates are both functional and fashionable and have many practical details. You can also wear them in the city, of course.

184 SNOW PEAK

5 **JEWELLERY** *shops*
by young designers

186 **TALKATIVE**

4-24-5 Jingumae
Shibuya-ku ③
+81 (0)3-6416-0559
talkative.jp

Talkative's designer Shinobu Marotta creates pieces of jewellery that boost your energy and make you feel more optimistic in everyday life. Some of the rings with gemstones are unique, one-off items, so if you find one that fits your finger, it might well be your destiny!

187 MONAKA JEWELLERY

3-14-26 Minami-
Aoyama
Minato-ku ④
+81 (0)3-6434-7816
monakajewellery.com

Asako Hojin, the designer of MONAKA, collects rare gemstones and diamonds from all over the world to make hand-made pieces. One of her lines, called 'Rock', is a real eye-catcher, as the designer makes a bold use of natural stones.

188 SIMMON

18-5 Uguisudani
Shibuya-ku ①
+81 (0)3-6455-3467
simmon-s.com

The atelier and shop of the young Japanese jewellery designer Shimon Sato, whose works are sold in shops in and outside of Japan, including at the MoMA. He creates works with tiny animal motifs, including wolf and deer, which are totally cute. Drop him an e-mail first to see whether he is in.

189 SHIHARA

3-12-13 Kita-Aoyama
Minato-ku ③
+81 (0)3-6427-5503
shihara.com

Shihara is known for its minimalism and three-dimensional design. You may wonder how anyone can wear these stunning jewels, which are shaped like spirals, cuboids, or triangular pyramids. But despite their eccentric shapes, they are simple and elegant, pairing well with any style. Also available at Dover Street Market Ginza.

190 CHERRY BROWN

3-20-2 Higashi
Shibuya-ku ②
+81 (0)3-3409-9227
cherry-brown.com

Every piece at Cherry Brown is simple and understated, making them great for layering and stacking. Their collection, inspired by Origami, is a superb mix of of pearls and thin gold bars. Very cool and very Japanese.

5
DESIGNER CLOTHES
shops

---

191 FACETASM

5-4-30 Minami-
Aoyama
Minato-ku ④
+81 (0)3-6459-2223
facetasm.jp

The designer Hiromichi Ochiai established this brand in 2007. His creations soon caught the eye of the fashion-conscious crowd. Every item he designs has a distinctive shape, sometimes he adds cute frills. May not work as a head-to-toe look for you, but perhaps one item may be a good addition to your wardrobe?

192 FUMITO GANRYU

AT: ELIMINATOR
26-13 Sarugakucho
Shibuya-ku ②
+81 (0)3-3464-8144
online.fumitoganryu.jp

Ganryu started his career as a pattern maker at Junya Watanabe. In 2008, he became the youngest designer to have his own line, called GANRYU, under the COMME des GARÇONS umbrella. He launched Fumito Ganryu in 2018. The clothes he creates are both three-dimensional and chic.

193 UNDERCOVER

5-3-22 Minami-
Aoyama
Minato-ku ④
+81 (0)3-3407-1232
undercoverism.com

The Japanese designer Jun Takahashi established this brand while he was still in fashion college. As he only produced limited editions of his clothes, Undercover soon had a cult following. The collaboration with Nike Gyakusou is very popular with fashion-conscious runners.

194 DOVER STREET MARKET GINZA

6-9-5 Ginza
Chuo-ku ⑧
+81 (0)3-6228-5080
*ginza.dover
streetmarket.com*

Dover Street Market is a fashion department store run by COMME des GARÇONS, and this is their Ginza outlet. As well as CdG's brands, including Junya Watanabe and Noir Kei Ninomiya, they also stock many renowned brands, such as Balenciaga and Louis Vuitton. Pop over to the Rose Bakery on the seventh floor for some cake to give your feet a rest after all the shopping.

195 HYKE

AT: ISETAN RE-STYLE
3-14-1 Shinjuku
Shinjuku-ku ⑧
+81 (0)3-3352-1111
hyke.jp

A Japanese brand that attracts attention from all over the world. It was launched in 2013 by two Japanese designers who had already worked in the fashion industry. They use primary colours, such as khaki and black, and while their designs are simple, they are never boring.

5 not-to-miss
V I N T A G E *shops*

---

196 **EVA**

Avenue side
Daikanyama 1B
2-1 Sarugakucho
Shibuya-ku ①
+81 (0)3-5489-2488
evafashionart.com

The owner believes vintage clothes play a vital part in today's fashion industry. In fact, fashionable people like to mix vintage items with clothes from high fashion brands. The items EVA sells are all in mint condition and will look good in any wardrobe.

197 **TOGA XTC**

6-31-10 Jingumae
Shibuya-ku ③
+81 (0)3-6419-8136
toga.jp/store

The vintage clothes shop of the Japanese brand Toga's designer Yasuko Furuta. Located in the parking lot of Toga's Harajuku shop. This small shop stocks plenty of dresses, bags, shoes, and accessories from the seventies and eighties.

198 **VELVET**

AT: SUZURAN BUILDING
3-26-3 Kitazawa
Setagaya-ku ⑫
+81 (0)3-6407-8770
velvet.pw

The owner used to work as an editor. Although he had no previous experience as a clothes buyer or a shop owner, he has always worn vintage clothes. So he selects items from a (former) editor's point of view. Mainly for men, but women can also wear the stuff he sells if they like an oversized look.

199 DAIDAI

4-22-1 Koenji-Minami
Suginami-ku ⑬
+81 (0)3-3315-7191

Raggedy Ann & Andy, Smiley Face, teddy bears, animal motifs, etc. This shop is like the toyboxes in fantasy films, selling dresses with frills and the kind of floral print blouses that many children dream of.

200 LEMONTEA

6-11-8 Jingumae
Shibuya-ku ③
+81 (0)3-5467-2407
blog.lemontea-tokyo.net

From Nike vintage trainers to Harris Tweed jackets, they stock a variety of basic standard items from the United States and Europe. Vintage outdoor clothes that are wearable in the city and look cool. All items mix and match nicely with your non-vintage items.

199 DAIDAI

5 great places to
BUY A KIMONO

---

201 OYAMA KIMONO C'ERA UNA VOLTA

3-14-9 Minami-
Aoyama
Minato-ku ④
+81 (0)3-3479-8045
oyamakimono-shop.net

Located on a back street in Aoyama, they sell good quality antique kimonos. They also offer kimono-wearing lessons if you decide to buy one for yourself. Or you can ask them to help dress you. They also sell original *obi* (belts) made from import fabrics.

202 KIMONO HAZUKI

2-2-24 Izumi
Suginami-ku ⑫
+81 (0)3-6265-8734

The place to browse for colourful and fashionable antique and second-hand kimonos. The designs look so modern that you'll find it very hard to believe that some of these kimonos were made 100 years ago! Pick up a matching bag and *zori* (Japanese sandals) before you go.

203 SETAGAYA BORO ICHI

Setagaya
Setagaya-ku ⑬

The ultimate place to buy kimonos. Setagaya Boro Ichi is a flea market that has been held in December and January of every year since 1578. *Boro* means 'worn-out' and *ichi* is an abbreviation of *ichiba* (market). Who knows, you may even be able to score some bargains here.

204 **TOKYO HOTARUDO**

1-41-8 Asakusa
Taito-ku ⑩
+81 (0)3-3845-7563
tokyohotarudo.com

The place to go for vintage clothes. They have many items of the Taisho period (1912-1926). The kimonos of that era are quite colourful and fashionable and you can wear boots with them. They have accessories to go with the kimono.

205 **TANSUYA**

AT: NAKAYAMA BUILDING
3-4-5 Ginza
Chuo-ku ⑧
+81 (0)3-3561-8529
tansuya.jp

Tansuya is a used kimono shop. At their Ginza shop, you can buy kimonos for formal occasions. Try this shop if you are serious about purchasing a quality kimono (and are not on a budget).

5 must-visit
CONCEPT STORES

206 MAISON DE MARUYAMA

4-25-10 Minami-Aoyama
Minato-ku ④
+81 (0)3-3406-1935
keitamaruyama.com

The concept store of fashion designer Keita Maruyama where he creates something exciting and impressive. Here you'll find his collection and that of other designers he likes as well as tableware, furniture, and books. His studio is upstairs, so you can find him in the shop from time to time.

207 BEST PACKING STORE

1-23-5 Aobadai
Meguro-ku ②
+81 (0)3-5773-5586
bestpackingstore.com

The theme of this shop is 'travel'. Everything in this shop is designed to make your journey more comfortable and some of the products on sale are originals. The kind of shop that makes you want to go on a trip, but many of the items can be used every day even when you are not travelling.

208 ARCHIVE STORE

AT: WAKO BUILDING, B1
1-12-16 Jinnan
Shibuya-ku ①
+81 (0)3-5428-3787
archivestore.jp

They stock secondhand clothes from the 1990s to the 2000s, by world-famous brands such as COMME des GARÇONS, Maison Martin Margiela, and Yohji Yamamoto. These clothes have inspired many promising young designers. Even if you cannot afford them, it is worth visiting this store, which is very much like a museum.

209 **AKOMEYA TOKYO IN LA KAGŪ**

67 Yaraicho
Shinjuku-ku ⑤
+81 (0)3-5946-8241
akomeya.jp

AKOMEYA is all about 'sharing.' They have several shops in Tokyo, and this one in Kagurazaka is their flagship store, which opened in March 2019. You really should visit it, if you are interested in buying the ingredients for Japanese cuisine. The restaurant serves dishes made with the products in the shop.

210 **TSUTAYA ELECTRICS**

AT: TERRACE MARKET,
FUTAKO TAMAGAWA RISE
1-14-1 Tamagawa
Setagaya-ku ⑬
+81 (0)3-5491-8550
real.tsite.jp/
futakotamagawa

A consumer electronics shop, but not anything like the ones you'll find in Akihabara or Shinjuku. Here you shop for ultra-stylish electronics, as well as interior design items and books. The shop assistants are called 'concierges' and are experts in electronics.

The 5 best
INTERIOR DESIGN *shops*

211 FRANCFRANC
3-1-3 Minami-Aoyama
Minato-ku ④
+81 (0)3-4216-4021
francfranc.com

The flagship store of the popular interior design shop chain Francfranc. They sell products that will enrich your life, including their own original design range. Masterrecipe, one of their brands, offers simple but well-designed products that you can use for years. Fancy buying a towel made in Imabari?

215 LIVING MOTIF

212 IDÉE

2-16-29 Jiyugaoka
Meguro-ku ⑬
+81 (0)3-5701-7555
idee.co.jp

They originally started out as an imported furniture shop in 1975, but now they sell original, well-made furniture that lasts a lifetime. Their designs are timeless and add instant warmth to your interior. The Bakeshop, on the fourth floor, exudes the same fuzzy warmth.

213 D&DEPARTMENT TOKYO

8-3-2 Okusawa
Setagaya-ku ⑬
+81 (0)3-5752-0120
d-department.com

A 1000-square-metre emporium that stocks furniture, housewares, books, and CDs. Some of the products are second-hand. They also organise workshops, on knife sharpening for example, inviting professionals, and a farmer's market.

214 JOURNAL STANDARD FURNITURE

AT: G BUILDING SHIBUYA 01
1-20-13 Jinnan
Shibuya-ku ①
+81 (0)3-5728-5355

An interior design shop, which is run by the popular select shop Journal Standard. They sell a mix of trendy and vintage items from Japan and other countries. They also offer a full renovation service, and will even start by finding you a home. You can start with one room if you have no intention just yet of buying a home.

215 LIVING MOTIF

5-17-1 Roppongi
Minato-ku ⑥
+81 (0)3-3587-2784
livingmotif.com

Design-conscious people have been flocking to shop for more than four decades, which stocks a nice selection of furniture, kitchen goods, and stationery from inside and outside Japan. If you're looking for a cool gift, this shop would be a good place to start.

5 nice
C R A F T *shops*

---

216 **HANDS**

12-18 Udagawacho
Shibuya-ku ①
+81 (0)3-5489-5111
hands.net

The department store of creative people's dreams, selling everything from stationery to hardcore DIY tools. The staff are knowledgeable and helpful. On the 6th floor, they stock a variety of fabrics and leathers. There is a cafe on the seventh floor. Easy to see how you could spend the whole day here...

217 **YUZAWAYA**

8-23-5 Nishi-Kamata
Ota-ku ⑭
+81 (0)3-3734-4141
yuzawaya.co.jp

If you are a keen knitter, then head over to this department store, which sells a variety of knitting yarns. They also have fabrics, beads, and other crafts goods. They sometimes organise free in-store craft workshops. Register online if you are interested.

218 **OKADAYA**

3-23-17 Shinjuku
Shinjuku-ku ⑦
+81 (0)3-3352-5411
okadaya.co.jp

A large craft shop in Shinjuku. Here they sell everything you need for crafts, including fabrics, buttons, and ribbons, as well as make-up goods for the stage and wigs. Some of the shop assistants can advise you on how to make your own costume for cosplay.

219 TOA

1-19-3 Jinnan
Shibuya-ku ①
+81 (0)3-3463-3351
toa-ltd.com

This fabric shop is stocked to the rafters with bargain items. Some of the fabrics often sell for less than 200 yen a metre. Most people go there to buy colourful fake fur. Fabrics with cute patterns, stylish and sophisticated textiles… a place that will fuel your creativity.

220 TSUYOSE

5-66-5 Nakano
Nakano-ku ⑫
+81 (0)3-3387-6231
tsuyose.wixsite.com/
tsuyosenakano

A shop that stocks reasonably-priced clothing fabrics, yarn, buttons, thread, and other handicraft materials. Their selections of yarn, available year-round (even in summer!), is excellent. They also organise knitting workshops!

5 of the best
DEPA-CHIKA
(food halls)

---

221 ISETAN SHINJUKU STORE

3-14-1 Shinjuku
Shinjuku-ku ⑦
+81 (0)3-3352-1111
isetan.mistore.jp

Isetan Shinjuku is probably the busiest department store in Tokyo as several shops sell limited products there. The cookies by Fika, produced by Isetan Mitsukoshi Holdings, are especially popular. They are beautifully packed, making them the perfect gift.

222 HIKARIE

2-21-1 Shibuya
Shibuya-ku ①
+81 (0)5468-5892
hikarie.jp

Many of the products are only available from Hikarie but fortunately they are not as busy as Isetan. The basement cafe is overseen by the world's top barista Paul Bassett with Japan's leading patissier Yoshihiro Tsujiguhi. The only place in the world where you can find this combo of coffee and pastries.

223 IKEBUKURO SEIBU

1-28-1 Minami-
Ikebukuro
Toshima-ku ⑪
+81 (0)3-3981-0111
sogo-seibu.jp/
ikebukuro

Their food hall is huge. They even have guides on hand to point you in the right direction: 'delica attendant' and 'sweets attendant'. Just tell them what kind of deli food or sweets you are looking for and they will help you. There are eat-in spaces where you can have sushi, *soba*, or tempura.

224 TOKYU FOOD SHOW

AT: MARK CITY 1ST &
B1 FLS / SHIBU-CHIKA
1-12-1 Dogenzaka
Shibuya-ku ①
+81 (0)3-3477-3111
tokyu-dept.co.jp/
tokyufoodshow

In 2021, Tokyu Food Show reopened after a refurb, expanding their sales floor. The atmosphere here is slightly different compared with other *depa-chika:* the sales floor in this food hall is always lively and looks like a 'real' fish market. Don't forget to check out the amazing sweets zone on the first floor.

225 GINZA SIX

6-10-1 Ginza
Chuo-ku ⑧
+81 (0)3-6891-3390
ginza6.tokyo

This food hall opened in 2017 and is possibly the most luxurious *depa-chika* in Japan, with world-famous shops and famous shops from all over Japan. Several of the products are 'only available at Ginza Six'. One of their most popular shops is the *noriben* (bento with rice covered with seasoned *nori* seaweed) shop. Join the line outside?

224 TOKYU FOOD SHOW

The 5 best
JAPANESE SWEET
shops

---

226 HIGASHIYA MAN

3-17-14 Minami-
Aoyama
Minato-ku ④
+81 (0)3-5414-3881
higashiya.com

They have *kashi* (sweets) that can be served with Japanese tea. They offer freshly steamed buns all through the year as well as *aisu monaka* (red bean ice cream in rice wafers) in summer and *oshiruko* (hot red bean soup) in winter.

227 QUOLOFUNE

1-24-11 Jiyugaoka
Meguro-ku ⑬
+81 (0)3-3725-0038
quolofune.com

Kasutera is a type of sponge cake made with flour, eggs and sugar. This Portuguese sweet was first introduced to Japan during the Edo period. Their *kasutera* is very airy with a fine texture, and their rusks, made of *kasutera*, are so crunchy that you won't stop at one.

228 MIZUHO

6-8-7 Jingumae
Shibuya-ku ③
+81 (0)3-3400-5483

Located on a back street in busy Harajuku, they sell only two things here: *mame daifuku*, *mochi* stuffed with red bean paste, and *monaka*, wafers filled with bean paste. Their *daifuku* is especially famous, and they often sell out before midday, even on weekdays.

229 KAMEJU

2-18-11 Kaminarimon
Taito-ku ⑩
+81 (0)3-3841-2210

Do you know the Japanese anime *Doraemon*? Do you remember what Doraemon likes to eat? *Dorayaki* of course! This snack is made with two small pancakes, stuffed with bean paste and is a popular sweet for Japanese people, but Kameju's *dorayaki* has a softer texture than others. There is always a line, but you'll find out soon enough that it's worth the wait.

230 KASHO SHOAN

1-9-20 Hiroo
Shibuya-ku ②
+81 (0)3-3441-1822

Their products are only sold at a few locations in Tokyo, which is why people often buy them as a gift when they visit people, friends and families outside Tokyo. *Anzu Daifuku*, *mochi* stuffed with red bean paste and apricot, is one of their signature products.

228 MIZUHO

The 5 best
PATISSERIES

231 **EN VEDETTE**

2-1-3 Miyoshi
Koto-ku ⑮
+81 (0)3-5809-9402
envedette.jp

Pâtissier Daisuke Mori was trained in Tokyo and Paris and has won world-famous competitions. The cakes he creates are cute, colourful, and delicious! The 'Petit Livre Kuchen,' with *pâte de fruits* between *Baumkuchen,* make a nice gift for book lovers.

234 SHIROTAE

232 AU BON VIEUX TEMPS

2-1-3 Todoroki
Setagaya-ku ⑬
+81 (0)3-3703-8428
aubonvieuxtemps.jp

One of the most renowned French patisseries by a Japanese patissier. Even French people who live in Tokyo recommend this shop. Their *gateaux secs* (biscuits) are very popular as a gift. They have an eat-in space where you can have lunch as well as cakes, of course.

233 GONDOLA

3-7-8 Kudan-Minami
Chiyoda-ku ⑤
+81 (0)3-3265-2761
patisserie-gondola.com

Their pound cake is widely considered the best in Tokyo. The shop opened over 80 years ago and its popularity has remained unchanged. As they are located in a business district, people often buy a box of their biscuits to present to clients.

234 SHIROTAE

4-1-4 Akasaka
Minato-ku ⑤
+81 (0)3-3586-9039

This shop opened in 1975 and its cheese-cake proved a hit from the start. The 'rare' cheesecake, or unbaked cheesecake, is made with cream cheese, sugar, and lemon and nothing else. It is quite small but very filling because it is so rich. Their *choux à la crème* are also popular.

235 SEIKOTEI

2-30-3 Uehara
Shibuya-ku ⑫
+81 (0)3-3468-2178
seikotei.jp

Their boxes are beautifully illustrated with squirrels and are so cute that people often buy their products as a gift. The illustrations are by a Japanese female illustrator who has been drawing squirrels for them for over 15 years. The cookies in the boxes are simply delicious.

5 essential

INTERNATIONAL FOOD

stores

---

236 KINOKUNIYA INTERNATIONAL

3-11-7 Kita-Aoyama
Minato-ku ③
+81 (0)3-3409-1231
super-kinokuniya.jp

They opened as Japan's very first super-market in 1953, selling a selection of products from all over the country as well as many imported foods and goods. Their in-store bakery sells a wide range of bread including German bread. Their original eco-bags are very robust and popular with customers.

237 NATIONAL AZABU

4-5-2 Minami-Azabu
Minato-ku ⑥
+81 (0)3-3442-3181
national-azabu.com

As this shop is located in an area where many expats live, you'll notice that they have many imported products you might not find at other stores. Since the 1960s, they have made the lives of many an expat in Tokyo much easier. About 70% of their customers are not Japanese.

238 SEIJO ISHII

2-27-25 Minami-Aoyama
Minato-ku ④
+81 (0)3-5786-2880
seijoishii.co.jp

This posh supermarket chain can be found throughout the Honshu area. Their selection of desserts, which includes baked puddings, cheesecakes, and *warabi mochi* (made from bracken starch), is hugely popular. Some branches, including this one and the ones in Jinbocho and Azabu Juban, are open 24 hours.

239 VILLE MARCHE

2-13-5 Kita-Aoyama
Minato-ku ④
+81 (0)3-3403-1677
ville-marche.jp

This shop opened in 2016 and mainly sells organic products. They have a partnership with about 100 farmers from whom they source good-quality seasonal products, and all of the agricultural products are traceable. They have an in-store bakery and freshly-brewed organic coffee. A good place to shop if you like healthy food.

240 KAWACHIYA SHOKUHIN

4-6-12 Ueno
Taito-ku ⑩
+81 (0)3-3831-2215
kawachiya-foods.com

Ameya Yokocho, aka Ameyoko, is an open-air market in Ueno and Kawachiya Shokuhin is one of the shops in the market. They import products from 30 countries around the world. If you're looking for a specific spice or herb, you may be able to find it here.

5 STALLS and FOOD TRUCKS at the UNU Farmer's Market

Farmer's Market at United Nations University
5-53-70 Jingumae
Shibuya-ku ③
farmersmarkets.jp

241 BUGRASS FARMERS

bugrassfarmers.jp

Their name 'Bugrass' is a combination of bug and grass. They supply natural, organic vegetables and fruits. Chefs from nearby restaurants and cafes visit to buy seasonal vegetables every weekend.

242 MIKANYA HIROSHI

Hiroshi Matsumoto sells a range of amazingly sweet and juicy citrus fruits from Wakayama prefecture. He often offers people a taster, so go ahead and try some of his lovely citrus. During the summer months, he also stocks gorgeously sweet peaches.

243 DANGOYA MORI

Dango is a type of Japanese dumpling made from rice flour. The dumplings are steamed, and three of them are skewered together and served with sweet pastes made of red beans, sesame, or sauce made of soy sauce and sugar. Try the edamame paste!

244 KOMESHIRUNA

Their van has been fitted with a firewood oven, which they use to cook rice and eggs, and grill meat. Have you ever tasted rice cooked in a stove instead of in an electric rice cooker? Try it with grilled pork, seasoned with salt and some sugar and nothing else.

245 SAUCE MANIA

*luro-foods.
amebaownd.com*

They sell raw vegan dressings made from seasonal vegetables and fruits. The dressings are used for salads as well as fish or meat dishes. They are so thick that you can use them even as a pasta sauce.

5
SPECIALIST SHOPS

246 KIYA
AT: COREDO MUROMACHI
2-2-1 Nihonbashi
Muromachi
Chuo-ku ⑧
+81 (0)3-3241-0110
kiya-hamono.co.jp

This shop, established in the 16th century, sells top-quality knives and scissors. They produce various chef's knives, from Japanese ones to Western and Chinese ones. Their gardening scissors and nail clippers are also popular. You can have your KIYA products sharpened here too.

247 OKUNO KARUTA
2-26 Kanda Jinbocho
Chiyoda-ku ⑨
+81 (0)3-3264-8031
okunokaruta.com

This shop specialises in Japanese playing cards, called *karuta*. *Karuta* derives from the Portuguese word *carta*, which were introduced in Japan by the Portuguese around the 1550s. This shop opened in 1921 and sells a variety of *karuta* and imported card games. They also regularly exhibit rare *karuta* sets.

248 HAIBARA
2-7-1 Nihonbashi
Chuo-ku ⑧
+81 (0)3-3272-3801
haibara.co.jp

This *washi* (traditional Japanese paper) shop opened in 1806. Of course, you can buy *washi* here but they also stock a variety of products made of *washi*, such as postcards, letter sets, and notebooks. *Chiyogami* (pattern-printed *washi*) is so beautiful that it wouldn't look out of place in a picture frame on a wall.

249 KAMAWANU

23-1 Sarugakucho
Shibuya-ku ②
+81 (0)3-3780-0182
kamawanu.co.jp

This shop sells *tenugui*, or Japanese hand towels made of cotton. Japanese people can't do without *tenugui* in everyday life. They dry very quickly so they can be used as tea towels as well. You will be amazed by the variety of colourful and fashionable designs they sell.

250 MATSUNEYA

2-1-10 Asakusabashi
Taito-ku ⑩
+81 (0)3-3863-1301
matsuneya.jp

A shop specialising in *sensu* (folding fan) and *uchiwa* (fan). The performers in the theatres in Asakusa and people who participate in festivals love their fans. If you're looking for more contemporary designs, look for the Showohdo brand, which was created by the current shop-keeper, a fourth-generation descendant of the shop's founder.

249 KAMAWANU

5 interesting
CD and VINYL SHOPS

251 DISCLAND JARO

26-6 Udagawacho
Shibuya-ku ①
+81 (0)3-3461-8256
www1.ttv.ne.jp/
disclandjaro

This shop, which opened in 1973, has always specialised in jazz. They have approximately 8000 records, mainly modern jazz, and you might come across some very rare discoveries in this tiny, ten-square-metre space. Please note that they do not accept credit cards.

252 JET SET TOKYO

2-33-12 #201 Kitazawa
Setagaya-ku ⑫
+81 (0)3-5452-2262
jetsetrecords.net

A popular shop with vinyl lovers as they produce records under their own label. The best place to score vinyl records by Japanese rock bands or hip-hop artists.

253 BONJOUR RECORDS

24-1 Sarugakucho
Shibuya-ku ②
+81 (0)3-5458-6020
bonjour.jp

One of the landmarks of Daikanyama area. One of the first shops to combine music with fashion, selling records and CDs as well as clothes including items from their original brand. They also have a cafe on the ground floor. A good place to start to explore the area.

254 FACE RECORDS

10-2 Udagawacho
Shibuya-ku ①
+81 (0)3-3462-5696
facerecords.com

You may think that this is a clothes shop based on its façade but this is actually a used record shop with an excellent selection of 7-inch and 12-inch vinyl. They specialise in jazz, soul, reggae, and various other kinds of world music. If the shop isn't too crowded, the friendly shop assistants will let you listen to records.

255 DISK UNION

AT: YAMADA BUILDING
3-31-4 Shinjuku
Shinjuku-ku ⑦
+81 (0)3-3352-2697
diskunion.net

Most of the Yamada building is occupied by Disk Union's shops, but each floor specialises in a particular genre, with Japanese Rock and Pop in the basement. If you are looking for City Pop CDs and records, do visit this floor.

255 DISK UNION

The 5 best
BOOKSHOPS

---

256 AOYAMA BOOK CENTER

AT: COSMOS AOYAMA,
GARDEN FLOOR B2F
5-53-67 Jingumae
Shibuya-ku ③
aoyamabc.jp

Possibly the best bookshop if you are looking for books on architecture, photography, and fine arts. Their shop is bright and airy, so you feel very comfortable while browsing their selection of books and magazines. They also organise small exhibitions and in-store events.

257 HMV & BOOKS SHIBUYA

AT: SHIBUYA MODI BUILDING
1-21-3 Jinnan
Shibuya-ku ①
+81 (0)3-5784-3270
hmv.co.jp

HMV's first shop complex, located on the 5th, 6th and 7th floors of Shibuya MODI building, in the heart of Shibuya. Each level has an event space, and around 1000 events, including live music performances and talk shows, are organised here every year. They have a good selection of subculture books.

258 MORIOKA SHOTEN

AT: SUZUKI BUILDING
1-28-15 Ginza
Chuo-ku ⑧
+81 (0)3-3535-5020
takram.com

This bookshop sells only one title every week. They will display a particular book (which you can buy) and exhibit and sell related items in the shop. They often invite the author of the book they chose during that specific week. It is like a salon where authors, editors, and readers can gather around a specific book.

259 VILLAGE VANGUARD

AT: SHIBUYA DAI-ICHI
KANGYO KYODO BUILDING,
B1&B2
23-3 Udagawacho
Shibuya-ku ①
+81 (0)3-6416-5641

A bookshop chain, which is very popular with creative people and subculture fans, selling books and magazines as well as goods that are featured in magazines. But be warned: once you cross that doorstep, you might find it very difficult to drag yourself out of there and you may even end up breaking the bank.

260 DAIKANYAMA TSUTAYA BOOKS

AT: DAIKANYAMA T-SITE
17-5 Sarugakucho
Shibuya-ku ②
+81 (0)3-3770-2525
real.tsite.jp/
daikanyama

Tsutaya created the concept of a 'cultural convenience store' with the Daikanyama T-Site, which is a new type of cultural complex facility. Daikanyama Tsutaya is located in the centre of the site. The place to go for books, films, and music and the kind of shop where you could happily spend hours browsing.

蔦屋書店
TSUTAYA BOOKS

5
STATIONERY
shops to check out

---

261 ITO-YA

2-7-15 Ginza
Chuo-ku ⑧
+81 (0)3-3561-8311
ito-ya.co.jp

Ito-ya, which opened in 1904, is a long-established stationery shop and reopened in 2015 after a renovation. The coffee counter on the ground floor starts serving at 8 am. You can buy and write postcards (you can even borrow a pen) in the Write & Post section on the second floor. There is even a post box!

264 KAKIMORI

262 LOFT

21-1 Udagawacho
Shibuya-ku ①
+81 (0)3-3462-3807
loft.co.jp

They sell a variety of products, including stationery as well as kitchen gadgets and interior design items but are mostly known for their amazing array of diaries and pens. From simple, practical ones to cute illustrated ones, they cater to every generation.

263 MARUZEN

AT: MARUNOUCHI OAZO,
1ST-4TH FL.
1-6-4 Marunouchi
Chiyoda-ku ⑧
+81 (0)3-5288-8881
maruzenjunkudo.co.jp

Maruzen is Japan's largest bookshop chain, and most of their branches also sell a vast range of stationary. This is the place to go if you're in the market for a new fountain pen! The expert staff will suggest the right model by looking at how you hold a pen and write.

264 KAKIMORI

1-6-2 Misuji
Taito-ku ⑩
+81 (0)50-1744-8546
kakimori.com/en

At this shop, you can blend your original ink and design your own customised notebook. Pick from 17 colours to mix your own, unique ink. The ink comes in the shop's original ink bottle, which is so attractive that you will want to put it on your desk.

265 GEKKOSO

8-7-2 Ginza
Chuo-ku ⑧
+81 (0)3-3572-5605
gekkoso.jp

An art supply store, which opened in 1917. They sell original paints (oil colour, watercolour, and gouache) and all the tools you need to paint. Every product features their horn logo. Their other original goods, such as pen cases and notebooks, are also very popular.

5

STATIONERY ITEMS

you should buy

---

266 FRIXION PENS

A series of erasable gel ink pens. There are 24 colours available in several thicknesses as well as highlighters, colour pencils, and stamps. They even have more professional models for businesspeople. Now that FriXion exists, kids no longer require correction fluid at school.

267 DECORESE PENS

A series of gel pens with a paint-like look and texture. A little bit like 3D. They come in lame and pastel colours and can be used on paper as well as plastic, glass, and metal. You can also use them for your nail art.

268 MECHANICAL PENCILS

Have you ever dreamed about a mechanical pencil with a lead that never breaks or doesn't need shaking for the lead to pop into place? They do exist. There is even a model with a rotating lead that sharpens itself every time you write. Japanese pencils are amazingly high tech.

269 COPIC MARKERS

Copic is a series of alcohol markers that are widely used by creative people including illustrators and architects. If you are not familiar with this series, you may want to consider buying the Copic Chao set of 36 colours. Then you can add other colours you like – there are 180 colours in all.

270 MASKING TAPE

Japanese people love to use masking tape as an alternative to Scotch tape but there are plenty of other fun uses. You can decorate a card, use it to stick a piece of paper in your diary, and so on. Some museum shops even sell special ones in the theme of their temporary exhibitions.

The 5 best
100 YEN / 300 YEN SHOPS

---

271 DAISO HARAJUKU
AT: VILLAGE 107, 2ND FL.
1-19-24 Jingumae
Shibuya-ku ③
+81 (0)3-5775-9641
daiso-sangyo.co.jp

The largest Daiso shop in Tokyo. If you are not familiar with Japan's 100 Yen shop concept, then start here. They have a variety of gifts for overseas tourists. It is known that talent scouts in the entertainment industry often stand in front of the shop in search of future actresses.

272 SERIA
AT: 17DIXSEPT, 3RD FL.
17-6 Daikanyamacho
Shibuya-ku ②
+81 (0)3-6416-1403
seria-group.com

Like the Daiso shop in Harajuku, this Seria shop is located in the heart of Daikanyama, one of the more fashionable areas in Tokyo. They have a good selection of products, catering to several generations. After spending time in this shop, there are plenty of places where you can have a coffee break nearby.

273 CANDO
AT: SEIBU SHINJUKU PEPE, 8TH FL.
1-30-1 Kabukicho
Shinjuku-ku ⑦
+81 (0)3-3202-1160
cando-web.co.jp

The largest Cando shop in Tokyo and the most extensive 100 Yen shop in Shinjuku area. The building is directly connected to Shinjuku Station, Seibu Shinjuku Line and is just a short walk from JR Shinjuku Station. They have a good selection of stationery.

274 3COINS

6-12-22 Jingumae
Shibuya-ku ③
+81 (0)3-6427-4333
3coins.jp

Every item costs less than 300 yen
(+ the value added tax) here. Perhaps,
their products are slightly cuter than
the products in the 100 Yen shops. The
accessories, including bags, hair clips,
and earrings, do not look like they only
cost 300 yen. They have a lot of useful
kitchen gadgets as well.

275 COUCOU

2-11-6 Jiyugaoka
Meguro-ku ⑬
+81 (0)3-6421-1358
coucou.co.jp

Another 300 Yen shop, which is very
popular with Japanese teenagers, who
like to buy many of their original items
including eco shoulder bags which sell
like hotcakes and make a good gift for
cycling fans. Their original kitchen
gadgets are also worth checking out.

ASAKUSA CULTURE TOURIST INFORMATION CENTER

15 NOTABLE BUILDINGS

5 *buildings* YOU CAN'T AFFORD TO MISS — 156

5 *great examples of*
MODERN ARCHITECTURE ———————— 158

5 *buildings* BY TADAO ANDO ———————— 160

5 buildings
YOU CAN'T AFFORD TO MISS

276 REVERSIBLE DESTINY LOFTS – MITAKA

2-2-8 Osawa
Mitaka-shi
rdloftsmitaka.com

Japan's super-aged society is ageing fast, which explains why there are so many 'barrier-free' residences for senior citizens. This, however, is an 'anti-barrier-free,' or anti-ageing apartment designed by artists Shusaku Arakawa and Madeline Gins. They built it because they believed barriers are instrumental to developing our skills.

277 RYOTEI

AT: KIYOSUMI GARDENS
3-3-9 Kiyosumi
Koto-ku ⑮
+81 (0)3-3461-5982

A *Sukiya-zukuri* style building, the style of which is influenced by the teahouse that was built in 1909 to welcome a British military leader of WWI, called Horatio Herbert Kitchener, during his inspection tour in Japan. Kiyosumi Teien is a leading example of a modern Japanese garden, and this Ryotei is a crucial element in it.

278 JIYUGAKUEN MYONICHIKAN

2-31-3 Nishi-Ikebukuro
Toshima-ku ⑪
+81 (0)3-3971-7535
jiyu.jp

This former school building was designed by famous American architect, Frank Lloyd Wright, in 1921. He received the commission while staying in Japan to design the Imperial Hotel. It is listed as a cultural property of national importance. Along with the Imperial Hotel, this is regarded as Wright's most important work in Japan.

279 SHIZUOKA SHIMBUN AND SHIZUOKA BROADCASTING SYSTEM BUILDING

8-3-7 Ginza
Chuo-ku ⑧

This building is the Tokyo office of Shizuoka prefecture's regional newspaper and broadcasting companies. It was designed by Kenzo Tange and built in 1967. The design was influenced by the Metabolism trend. Catch a glimpse of it from the platform of JR Shimbashi Station while waiting for your train or even see it from the Yamanote Line.

280 SEKIGUCHI CATHOLIC CHURCH / ST MARY'S CATHEDRAL

3-16-15 Skiguchi
Bunkyo-ku ⑪
+81 (0)3-3945-0126
cathedral-sekiguchi.jp

This cathedral was also designed by Kenzo Tange. The previous building burnt down during WWII and was rebuilt with the support of the churches in Cologne, Germany, in 1964. From the outside, you would not guess that this is a church, but when seen from above, you realise that this is a cross-shaped building.

280 SEKIGUCHI CATHOLIC CHURCH

5 great examples of
MODERN
ARCHITECTURE

---

281 PRADA STORE

5-2-6 Minami-Aoyama
Minato-Ku ④
+81 (0)3-6418-0400
prada.com

Designed by the Swiss architects Herzog & de Meuron, this building really stands out in this area where you can shop for all the luxury brands. Don't forget to see it from the inside as well. You can also see the Miu Miu shop, designed by the same architects, through the rhomboid-shaped pattern on the façade.

281 PRADA STORE

282 MAISON HERMÈS

5-4-1 Ginza
Chuo-ku ⑧
+81 (0)3-3569-3300
maisonhermes.jp

Designed by Renzo Piano, this is the headquarters of Hermès Japon. During the day, the sun shines in through the glass façade, and at night, the same façade glows with the light from within. The Forum, on the eighth floor, hosts contemporary art exhibitions.

283 THE ICEBERG

6-12-18 Jingumae
Shibuya-ku ③

Designed by Creative Designers International, the Tokyo-based firm of the British architect Benjamin Warner. The concept behind the building's design is 'crystal cast out into an urban area'. It looks like an iceberg as the whole surface has a blueish metallic coating.

284 ASAKUSA CULTURE TOURIST INFORMATION CENTER

2-18-9 Kaminarimon
Taito-ku ⑩
+81 (0)3-3842-5566
city.taito.lg.jp

Designed by Kengo Kuma, an internationally-renowned Japanese architect. The building resembles seven tiers of wooden houses. Despite its very modern appearance, it blends in quite harmoniously with the surroundings. There is an observatory terrace on the eighth floor.

285 AOYAMA TECHNICAL COLLEGE

7-9 Uguisudanicho
Shibuya-ku ①
aoyamaseizu.ac.jp

You can study architecture and design at this professional technical college. Building 1 was designed by Makoto Sei Watanabe/Architect's Office who won the international competition in 1988. It is also referred to as 'Gundam Building', reminding people of the anime series.

5 buildings
BY TADAO ANDO

---

286 **21_21 DESIGN SIGHT**
AT: TOKYO MIDTOWN
9-7-6 Akasaka
Minato-ku ⑤
+81 (0)3-3475-2121
2121designsight.jp

Here people can broaden their understanding of design. The space is located in the Midtown Garden, right next to Hinokicho Park. You will somehow be inspired during your visit. In spring, you can also enjoy the cherry blossoms here.

287 **OMOTESANDO HILLS**
4-12-10 Jingumae
Shibuya-ku ③
+81 (0)3-3497-0310
omotesandohills.com

This building does not really look that special from the outside. Step inside, however, and you will soon be fascinated by its spiral ramp. This shopping centre was built on a wedge-shaped strip of land, forcing Ando to make the most of the land's features.

288 **LA COLLEZIONE**
6-1-3 Minami-
Aoyama
Minato-ku ④
lacollezione.net

Built in 1989, this building consists of three cubes and one circular cylinder. Walking inside of the building, you may feel like as if you are lost in a maze but you will be amazed at the amount of daylight. La Collezione is a multipurpose event space, which hosts press conferences and parties.

289 TOKYO ART MUSEUM

1-25-1 Sengawa-cho
Chofu-shi
+81 (0)3-3305-8686
tokyoartmuseum.com

This museum of fine arts, design and architecture opened in 2004 as part of an urban planning project in Sengawa. The area, about a five-minute walk from the station, is known as 'Sengawa Ando Street' and has several buildings designed by Ando.

290 SHIBUYA STATION

TOKYO TOYOKO LINE
2-21-13 Shibuya
Shibuya-ku ①

You may have already walked through this station without knowing who designed it. Perhaps it was too crowded, or you were too busy looking at your smartphone. Anyway, here is a work that you can observe with very little effort. An egg-shaped shell wraps around the atrium, with natural light flooding into the underground level. Quintessential Ando.

286 21_21 DESIGN SIGHT

45 PLACES TO DISCOVER TOKYO

5 places for **HARUKI MURAKAMI FANS** —— 164

5 areas where you can see
OUTDOOR SCULPTURES ——————— 166

5 beautiful **GARDENS** ————————— 168

5 **FREE OBSERVATORIES** —————— 170

5 **SAKE BREWERIES** you should visit——— 172

5 spots to experience
HOW CROWDED TOKYO IS —————— 174

5 spots to see **MOUNT FUJI** ————— 176

The 5 most attractive
NATURAL HOT SPRINGS —————— 178

5 **TOILETS** worth checking out ———— 180

5 places for
HARUKI MURAKAMI
FANS

291 AOYAMA

Minato-ku ④

Aoyama is, without doubt, the area that is most frequently associated with the author as he refers to it in his works quite often. It is referenced in one of the short stories in his recent collection *Men without Women* as well.

292 SENDAGAYA / GAIENMAE

Shibuya-ku / Minato-ku ④

If you have read his essays and interviews or articles about his life rather than his works, you may be aware that Murakami supports the Japanese baseball team, the Yakult Swallows. The Swallows' home stadium is located in this area, and sometimes he turns up for a game. Peter Cat, the jazz bar that he used to run, was also in the area.

293 YOTSUYA SANCHOME

Shinjuku-ku ⑤

In his latest work *Kishidancho Goroshi* (*Killing Commendatore*), the protagonist visits the area a few times as this is where his ex-wife works. Walk about 10 to 15 minutes to get to Yotsuya, which was featured in *Norwegian Wood*, where Toru and Naoko took a walk.

294 **KOKUBUNJI**

Kokubunji-shi

He opened the jazz bar Peter Cat here, with his wife Yoko, when he was still at university. Though it has since been renovated, there is an apartment called Maison Keyaki where he used to live. He probably never imagined he would one day be this famous while living there.

295 **HIROO**

Shibuya-ku / Minato-ku ⑥

Aomame, the protagonist of 1Q84, works at an expensive sports club in this area. It was also referenced in *Drive My Car*, one of the short stories in *Men without Women*. You can follow Aomame's footsteps towards the 'Willow House' or drive a car like the female driver did in the short story.

5 areas where you can see
OUTDOOR SCULPTURES

296 ROPPONGI HILLS

6-10-1 Roppongi
Minato-ku ⑥
+81 (0)3-6406-6000
roppongihills.com

There are several public artworks here: six works are overseen by the Mori Art Museum and three works were selected by the architect Fumihiko Maki. The eight-metre-tall rose, which was created by the German sculptor Iza Genzken, and Maman, by the French artist Louise Bourgeois, are definitely worth checking out.

299 MARUNOUCHI STREET GALLERY

297 TOKYO MIDTOWN

9-7-1 Akasaka
Minato-ku ⑤
+81 (0)3-3475-3100
www.tokyo-
midtown.com

Art critic Toshio Shimizu and curator Jean-Hubert Martin selected artworks from artists all over the world. One of these works, called *Myomu* by the Hokkaido-born artist Kan Yasuda, welcomes you here in the space between Midtown East and West. There are several artworks inside the buildings as well.

298 TOKYO INTERNATIONAL FORUM

3-5-1 Marunouchi
Chiyoda-ku ⑧
+81 (0)3-5221-9000
www.t-i-forum.co.jp

There is one artwork on the site, called *Ishinki* and created by Kan Yasuda. He created several sculptures with the same name. There is another in Tokyo Midtown (but they are not the same shape). This work stands out between the geometric buildings.

299 MARUNOUCHI STREET GALLERY

Marunouchi
Naka-Dori
Chiyoda-ku ⑧

You can see several sculptures on Marunouchi Naka-Dori street, between the Tokyo International Forum and Tokyo Metro Otemachi Station, and a few around the Mitsubishi Ichigokan Museum. The gallery was created in 1972 to enrich people's lives. The sculptures definitely make us feel more upbeat.

300 FUCHUNOMORI PARK

1-3-1 Sengencho
Fuchu-shi
+81 (0)42-364-8021

You'll find a large number of sculptures in this park, especially around the Fuchu Art Museum. Most of them are by prominent Japanese sculptors, including Yasutake Funakoshi and Churyo Sato. Don't forget to look out for *Jackass and Elephant*, a work by the British-born sculptor Bally Flanagan.

5 beautiful
GARDENS

301 **RIKUGIEN GARDENS**
6-16-3 Hon-
Komagome
Bunkyo-ku ⑩
+81 (0)3-3941-2222

One of the best spots to see weeping cherry trees. Every year at the end of March, the mesmerising blossoms attract huge crowds. But spring is not the only season to enjoy this garden. Visit it in late November and you will be amazed by the bright red autumn leaves.

302 **HAPPO-EN**
1-1-1 Shirokanedai
Minato-ku ⑭
+81 (0)570-064-128
happo-en.com

People often book Happo-en for wedding ceremonies. You can also visit their garden, which has a tearoom where you can enjoy a cup of *matcha* with a seasonal Japanese sweet. Part of their building was apparently used as a model for Hayao Miyazaki's *Spirited Way*.

303 **HAMARIKYU GARDENS**
1-1 Hamarikyu Teien
Chuo-ku ⑮
+81 (0)3-3541-0200

One of the gardens used to be owned by a feudal lord during the Edo period. It is listed as a Japanese site of historic relevance and a place of scenic beauty. The water that runs through and around the garden comes directly from the sea. You may even spot jellyfish and other sea creatures swimming in it.

304 HANAHATA KINEN TEIEN

4-40-1 Hanahata
Adachi-ku

This garden was built to teach visitors about traditional Japanese culture.
The rooms at Oukatei, the building in the garden, can be hired for a wedding, ikebana, and many other purposes. It has a surface area of over 9000 square metres, and somehow reminds us of a castle in the Edo period.

305 SHINJUKU GYOEN NATIONAL GARDEN

11 Naitomachi
Shinjuku-ku ⑦
+81 (0)3-3350-0151
env.go.jp/garden/
shinjukugyoen

A place where you can see flowers throughout the year, including cherry blossoms in spring, crape myrtles in summer, autumn leaves in hues of red and gold, and plum blossoms in winter. There are a restaurant and a tearoom inside the garden to satisfy those hunger pangs. Neither serves alcohol, however, as consuming alcohol in the garden is prohibited.

305 SHINJUKU GYOEN NATIONAL GARDEN

5
FREE OBSERVATORIES

306 **TOKYO METROPOLITAN GOVERNMENT BUILDING OBSERVATION DECKS**

2-8-1 Nishi-Shinjuku Shinjuku-ku ⑦
+81 (0)3-5320-7890
metro.tokyo.jp

This observatory is located on the 45th floor of the Tokyo Metropolitan Government Office Building. It opens on weekends even though the offices are closed. A great place to enjoy unobstructed views of Tokyo from 202 metres above the ground. There is a direct lift to the observatory from the ground floor.

306 TOKYO METROPOLITAN GOVERNMENT BUILDING OBSERVATON DECKS

307 SKY LOUNGE

AT: YEBISU GARDEN
PLACE TOWER
4-20 Ebisu
Shibuya-ku ②
+81 (0)3-5423-7111
gardenplace.jp

This observatory is located in Yebisu Garden Place, which is a complex of commercial facilities built on the site of a former beer brewery. The lounge is located on the 38th and 39th floors. On a clear day you may even be able to spot Mount Fuji.

308 HIKARIE

2-21-1 Shibuya
Shibuya-ku ①
+81 (0)3-5468-5892
hikarie.jp.e.ui.
hp.transer.com

Hikarie is situated in one of Tokyo's busiest areas, Shibuya. There is no real observatory here but you can visit the observation area on the 11th floor. From here, the town of Shibuya looks like a diorama. Open until midnight.

309 BUNKYO CIVIC CENTER

1-16-21 Kasuga
Bunkyo-ku ⑩
+81 (0)3-5803-1162

This facility is owned by Bunkyo City. On a beautiful day, you can see the skyscrapers in Shinjuku area as well as Mount Tsukuba and Mount Fuji. There is a restaurant, a cafe, and a concert hall in the same building.

310 SKY CARROT OBSERVATORY

AT: CARROT TOWER
4-1-1 Taishido
Setagaya-ku ⑬
+81 (0)3-5430-1185

This free observatory is located on the 26th floor of a high-rise building, which you can enter from Sangenjaya Station. It is open until 11 pm and has a restaurant on the same floor so you can enjoy dinner with a view.

5

SAKE BREWERIES
you should visit

---

311 TOKYO PORT BREWERY

4-7-10 Shiba
Minato-ku ⑥
+81 (0)3-3451-2626
tokyoportbrewery.
wkmty.com

They started making sake here at the only sake brewery in the centre of Tokyo in 2016. In 2018, they opened the shop in front of the brewery where you can sample their products. Palla-Casey tastes like wine and pairs nicely with western dishes. Please note that you cannot visit the brewery itself.

312 TOSHIMAYA SHUZO

3-14-10 Kumegawacho
Higashimurayama-shi
+81 (0)42-391-0601
toshimayasyuzou.co.jp

They have been making sake here since 1596, during the Edo period. Their signature sake, Kinkon (which means 'golden wedding'), was launched on the occasion of the Meiji Emperor's silver wedding anniversary. You can buy Kinkon and other sake from their shop in Ochanomizu.

313 ISHIKAWA SHUZO

1 Kumagawa
Fussa-shi
+81 (0)42-553-0100
tamajiman.co.jp

This place styles itself as a 'theme park for sake lovers'. They offer a tour (available in English) so you can learn more about the sake brewing process and their buildings, parts of which are listed as cultural heritage. Don't forget to sample their sake, called Tamajiman, before leaving.

314 OZAWA SHUZO

2-770 Sawai
Ome-shi
+81 (0)42-878-8215
sawanoi-sake.com

They have been brewing sake here since 1702 and their signature brand, Sawanoi, is very well-known in Japan. You even have an opportunity to taste it during the brewery tour. Alternatively pop into one of the onsite restaurants. They also have a barbecue area.

315 TAMURA SHUZOJO

626 Fussa
Fussa-shi
+81 (0)42-551-0003
seishu-kasen.com

The Tamura family has been living in this area for over 400 years. In 1822, the ninth head of the family started to brew his own sake. In addition to their signature brand Kasen, they now also make Tamura, which was formulated by the current head of the family. Some parts of the brewery premises are listed as cultural heritage.

313 ISHIKAWA SHUZO

5 spots to experience
HOW CROWDED TOKYO IS

316 SHIBUYA SCRAMBLE CROSSING

Shibuya-ku ①

Everyone sooner or later ends up at this spot in Tokyo. An estimated 500.000 people use this crossing every day. The view from the Starbucks on the second floor of Shibuya Tsutaya, which faces the crossing, is quite amazing.

317 SHINJUKU STATION

Shinjuku-ku /
Shibuya-ku
⑦

The most crowded station in the world, which is used by an estimated 760.000 people every day. JR, Tokyo Metro, Toei subway, Odakyu, and Keio all stop at this station. There are another two stations, Shinjuku Sanchome and Seibu Shinjuku, within walking distance. Easy to see why it is so crowded.

318 IKEBUKURO STATION

Toshima-ku ⑪

Ikebukuro is the second most crowded station around the world. The large Sunshine City shopping centre has an aquarium, planetarium, theatre, and museum. The Nanja Town and J-World Tokyo amusement parks, which are both run by Namco, are also nearby, which explains why it can be so busy.

319 TOKYO METRO TOZAI LINE

The congestion rate around 8 am between Kiba and Monzennakacho is a whopping 200%. It's difficult to explain what this feels like but imagine being in a crammed underground, with so many passengers around you that you can barely see the screen of your phone. Most people are exhausted before they even make it to the office.

320 JR SOBU LINE

The congestion rate shops short of 200% during the morning rush hour between Kinshicho and Ryogoku. Many people prefer to commute into work much earlier so they can actually find a seat on the train and relax. That said, this line is always pretty crowded during the rush hour.

316 SHIBUYA SCRAMBLE CROSSING

5 spots to see
MOUNT FUJI

321 TAMAGAWA SENGEN SHRINE

1-55-12 Denen Chofu
Ota-ku ⑭
+81 (0)3-3721-4050
sengenjinja.info

Sengen Shrine was built more than 800 years ago during the Kamakura period. This ancient shrine is associated with the culture of faith relating to Mount Fuji and the mountain's spirit in particular. It is actually situated on an ancient burial mound, and a good place to enjoy a beautiful view of the mountain on a clear day.

324 MOUNT FUJI SEEN FROM RAINBOW BRIDGE

322 FUJIMI BRIDGE

Setagaya-ku ⑫

Many people visit this bridge in Seijo Gakuen, Setagaya-ku in early February because you can see 'diamond Fuji'. This stunning natural phenomenon occurs when the sun aligns with the summit of Mount Fuji at sunrise or sunset, causing the mountain to shine bright like a diamond.

323 HANEDA AIRPORT INTERNATIONAL PASSENGER TERMINAL

2-6-5 Haneda Kuko
Ota-ku ⑭
+81 (0)3-5757-8111
haneda-airport.jp/inter

You'll catch plenty of plane spotters on the observation deck on the fifth floor but it is also a good place for an unobstructed view of Mount Fuji. Realistically speaking, you should be able to see it from anywhere in Tokyo but the tall buildings often tend to get in the way. The view from Terminal 1 is also quite good.

324 RAINBOW BRIDGE

Minato-ku ⑭ ⑮

This 798-metre-long bridge was opened to connect Shibaura with Odaiba in 1993. You can cross the bridge by car or use the Yurikamome, a driverless, automated transit service. There is also a free foot-path. You might run into people with a tripod who are trying to get a perfect shot of Mount Fuji.

325 OYAMADA RYOKUCHI PARK

Shimo-
Oyamadamachi /
Kami-
Oyamadamachi
Machida-shi
+81 (0)42-797-8968

If you are lucky, you may be in town to witness Diamond Fuji, a phenomenon whereby the rising or setting sun aligns with the peak of Mount Fuji. This happens twice a year. You can only catch Diamond Fuji in some spots from where you can see the mountain.

The 5 most attractive
NATURAL HOT SPRINGS

---

326 MIYAGIYU

2-18-11 Nishi-
Shinagawa
Shinagawa-ku ⑭
+81 (0)3-3491-4856
miyagiyu.co.jp

A natural hot spring bath house near Shinagawa. Their hot spring naturally contains metasilicic acid which is said to beautify your skin. One of their two baths is on the rooftop, meaning you can gaze at the stars while enjoying a relaxing bath and getting lost in your thoughts. The men's and women's baths are replaced every week.

327 MYOJIN-NO-YU

1-18-1 Oyata
Adachi-ku
+81 (0)3-5613-2683
myoujin-no-yu.com

This *onsen* has several types of baths, a sauna, a massage parlour, and a restaurant (this is what we call a 'super sento'). The largest bath contains plenty of iron and salt, and is said to improve dermatological ailments. They provide rental body and hand towels.

328 TOKYO SOMEI ONSEN SAKURA

5-4-24 Komagome
Toshima-ku ⑪
+81 (0)3-5907-5566
sakura-2005.com/
english

This natural hot spring is located within walking distance of JR Sugamo station. They have indoor baths with a jacuzzi, open-air baths, and hot-stoned baths (for men and women). The water is amber in colour and is said to promote recovery from fatigue.

329 SHIMIZUYU

3-9-1 Koyama
Shinagawa-ku ⑭
+81 (0)3-3781-0575
shimizuyu.com

They have two springs here, the golden and the black spring. The water of the former is brought up from 1500 metres below the ground, from a layer that dates from the Pleistocene and contains enriched natural iodine. The latter one contains bicarbonate soda and plenty of minerals and is brought up from 200 metres. Both baths soften and moisturise your skin.

330 SAYA-NO-YUDOKORO

3-41-1 Maenocho
Itabashi-ku
+81 (0)3-5916-3826
sayanoyudokoro.co.jp

The pale green water in this bath house is pumped up straight from the source and is considered effective for those who suffer from neuralgia, muscle and joint pain, skin ailments and so on. There is a restaurant that serves *soba* noodles, made of 100% buckwheat without wheat flour.

5

TOILETS

worth checking out

---

331 HIKARIE

2-21-1 Shibuya
Shibuya-ku ①
+81 (0)3-5468-5892
hikarie.jp

The toilets at Hikarie are called Switch Rooms and they are not your usual run-of-the-mill toilets. There are six of them, and each one has a different concept with different lighting, BGM, and scent. If you have small kids with you, go to Mummy's STAGE in the basement (B2). Dad can use it, too.

332 HIGASHIYA GINZA

AT: POLA GINZA BUILDING,
2ND FL.
1-7-7 Ginza
Chuo-ku ⑧
+81 (0)3-3538-3230
higashiya.com/ginza

With a combination of black stone and plain wood, these women's toilets, and the wash basin especially, are just gorgeous. You will have to eat at the restaurant to use it but the experience is certainly worth it. Consider ordering a cup of tea and a piece of *yokan*, perhaps.

333 MANDARIN ORIENTAL TOKYO

2-1-1 Nihonbashi
Muromachi
Chuo-ku ⑧
+81 (0)3-3270-8800
mandarinoriental.co.jp/
tokyo

This hotel is located on floors 30 through 38 of the Nihonbashi Mitsui Tower and their lobby is on the 38th floor. So, if you have a chance to visit it, when you are staying or dining there, then do check out their toilet. People call it the 'toilet in the sky'.

334 LUMINE IKEBUKURO

1-11-1 Nishi-
Ikebukuro
Toshima-ku ⑪
+81 (0)3-5334-0550
lumine.ne.jp/
ikebukuro

Many people tend to use the toilets on the basement level of this building. But if you have some time to spare, then make the trek to the women's toilets on the 6th floor (sorry, guys). It is very bright and has plenty of space so you can touch up your make-up. In fact, you may even end up staying longer than you intended.

335 HOTEL GAJOEN TOKYO

1-8-1 Shimo-Meguro
Meguro-ku ⑭
+81 (0)3-3491-4111
hotelgajoen-tokyo.com

This hotel is considered to be one of most gorgeous places in the East and the same can definitely be said of their toilets, which resemble a tiny Japanese garden with a vermillion-lacquered bridge over a stream. The doors are decorated with mother-of-pearl while Japanese paintings cover the ceiling.

SHINJUKU SUEHIROTEI

55 PLACES TO ENJOY CULTURE

The 5 most beautiful **SHRINES** *and* **TEMPLES** — 184

5 places for **JAPANESE TRADITIONAL CULTURE** — 186

5 museums about **JAPANESE ART** — 188

5 interesting **SMALL MUSEUMS** — 191

5 **UNUSUAL MUSEUMS** — 193

5 must-do's at **KOKUGIKAN** — 196

5 essential places for **MANGA** *and* **ANIME LOVERS** — 198

5 **SPOTS** *you may have seen in* **FILMS** — 200

The 5 most interesting **FESTIVALS** *to catch* — 202

5 **FIREWORKS** *festivals not to miss* — 204

5 great **LIVE BARS** *and* **NIGHTCLUBS** — 206

The 5 most beautiful
SHRINES *and* TEMPLES

---

336 MANGANJI TEMPLE TODOROKI FUDOSON

1-22-47 Todoroki
Setagaya-ku ⑬
+81 (0)3-3701-5405
manganji.or.jp

Located close to Todoroki Keikoku, the only gorge in Tokyo's 23 wards, and a popular spot for *takigyo* or waterfall training. The more than 150 cherry trees here make for fantastic viewing spring. Stop for an ice cream at Shiki no Hana before leaving.

337 YASUKUNI SHRINE

3-1-1 Kudan-Kita
Chiyoda-ku ⑤
+81 (0)3-3261-8326
yasukuni.or.jp

This shrine was built by order of the Meiji Emperor in the late 19th century as a foundation for a peaceful Japan. There are major controversies surrounding this shrine, but let us forget about these for now and enjoy its beauty and the scenery of the cherry blossoms in spring and the red foliage in autumn.

338 GOHYAKURAKANJI

3-20-11 Shimo-
Meguro
Meguro-ku ⑭
+81 (0)3-3792-6751
rakan.or.jp

Rakan, or *arakan*, is called *arhat* in English and is a disciple of Buddha. At this temple, there are more than 300 statues of *arhat*. They are supposed to represent the 500 disciples who gathered at the death of Buddha. It is quite amazing to see such a large number of Buddhist statues gathered in one place.

339 KAMEIDO TENJIN
3-6-1 Kameido
Koto-ku ⑮
+81 (0)3-3681-0010
kameidotenjin.or.jp

There are more than 300 plum trees at this shrine, which are tended by Shinto priests. Ume Matsuri, or the Plum Festival, is held here from February to March when the trees are in blossom. The shrine is also known as a wonderful spot to see the wisteria flower in late April.

340 ZENPUKUJI
1-6-21 Moto-Azabu
Minato-ku ⑥
+81 (0)3-3451-7402
azabu-san.or.jpx

This temple was built in the 9th century, making it the third oldest temple in Tokyo. There is a huge 750-year-old gingko tree here with unusual branches, which all look like they are hanging down.

336 MANGANJI TEMPLE TODOROKI FUDOSON

5 places for
JAPANESE
TRADITIONAL CULTURE

---

341 **KABUKI-ZA THEATRE**
4-12-5 Ginza
Chuo-ku ⑧
+81 (0)3-3545-6800
kabuki-za.co.jp

This is one of the theatres where you can still attend traditional Kabuki performances. This unique Japanese theatre is over 400 years old. You can also enjoy a bento during the intermission. If you have a balcony seat, you can order a special bento, which will be delivered to your seat.

341 **KABUKI-ZA THEATRE**

342 NATIONAL THEATRE

4-1 Hayabusacho
Chiyoda-ku ⑤
+81 (0)3-3265-7411
ntj.jac.go.jp

Here you can see Kabuki, Noh, and Bunraku performances. The National Engei Hall, where you can enjoy story-telling performances, such as *rakugo*, *kodan*, and *rokyoku*, is located next to the National Theatre. There is also an exhibition space which showcases objects used in these traditional performing arts.

343 KANZE NOH THEATRE

AT: GINZA SIX
6-10-1 Ginza
Chuo-ku ⑧
+81 (0)3-6274-6579
kanze.net

One of the Noh theatres in Tokyo, which opened in 2017 in the basement of the Ginza Six commercial complex. Though it does not have any eating facilities, there are plenty of restaurants in the building and nearby. Check out their range of merchandise, which you can only buy here.

344 KIOI SMALL HALL

6-5 Kioicho
Chiyoda-ku ⑤
+81 (0)3-5276-4500
kioi-hall.or.jp

A concert hall for Japanese traditional music. The musicians play the *koto*, *shamisen*, and other traditional instruments and are sometimes accompanied by dancers. The hall, which can accommodate up to 250 people, is so small you can hear and almost feel the musicians breathing.

345 SHINJUKU SUEHIROTEI

3-6-12 Shinjuku
Shinjuku-ku ⑦
+81 (0)3-3351-2974
suehirotei.com

A venerable entertainment hall where traditional *rakugo* storytelling performances are given. Nowadays you can take in a *rakugo* performance almost anywhere, but this long-established theatre has been open since 1897 and is a great place to learn more about the world of *Showa Genroku Rakugo Shinju*, a serialised anime. You can bring food and drinks (but no alcohol).

5 museums about
JAPANESE ART

---

346 NEZU ART MUSEUM

6-5-1 Minami-
Aoyama
Minato-ku ④
+81 (0)3-3400-2536
nezu-muse.or.jp

The Japanese and oriental art collection of the businessman and politician Kaichiro Nezu (1860-1940). The museum reopened in 2009 after a three-year renovation. Take a walk in the lovely garden after visiting the collection for a break from the city in the city.

347 YAMATANE MUSEUM OF ART

3-12-36 Hiroo
Shibuya-ku ②
+81 (0)50-5541-8600
(NTT Hello Dial)
yamatane-museum.jp

This museum, which opened in 1966, specialises in Japanese art. Their collection includes several works that are listed as 'Important Cultural Properties', and which were created by Kagaku Murakami, Gyoshu Hayami, and several other leading artists. There is a cafe near the entrance where you can enjoy seasonal Japanese sweets.

348 OTA MEMORIAL MUSEUM OF ART

1-10-10 Jingumae
Shibuya-ku ③
+81 (0)50-5541-8600
(NTT Hello Dial)
ukiyoe-ota-muse.jp

Though this is not a large museum, it has an exciting collection of over 14.000 woodblock prints or ukiyo-e, including work by Hokusai and Hiroshige. During the summer, they usually host thematic exhibitions of ghost and monster prints.

349 **IDEMITSU MUSEUM OF ART**
AT: TEIGEKI BUILDING, 9TH FL.
3-1-1 Marunouchi Chiyoda-ku ⑧
+81 (0)50-5541-8600 (NTT Hello Dial)
idemitsu-museum.or.jp

This museum has a superb Japanese art collection, including *suiboku-ga* (monochrome ink painting) and Rimpa School paintings as well as Japanese calligraphy. The premises were designed by the architect Yoshio Taniguchi (who also designed an addition to the MoMA in NYC). One of the rooms originally was a tearoom and is now used as a gallery to display tea-making utensils.

350 **SEN-OKU HAKUKOKAN MUSEUM**
1-5-1 Roppongi Minato-ku ⑥
+81 (0)50-5541-8600 (NTT Hello Dial)
sen-oku.or.jp/tokyo

This museum, also known as the Sumitomo Collection, houses the collection of the family that founded this Japanese industrial conglomerate. The family has two museums. The other one is in Kyoto. The Tokyo museum exhibits utensils for the tea ceremony, ceramic art, Buddhist art, Noh masks and modern Japanese paintings.

346 NEZU ART MUSEUM

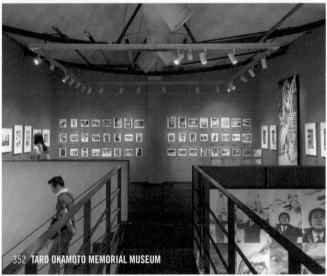

352 **TARO OKAMOTO MEMORIAL MUSEUM**

5 interesting
SMALL MUSEUMS

351 **KUMAGAI MORIKAZU MUSEUM**
2-27-6 Chihaya
Toshima-ku ⑪
+81 (0)3-3957-3779
kumagai-morikazu.jp

Morikazu Kumagai was a 20th-century Japanese artist. The museum was built on the site where he lived for 45 years. His highly-recognisable oil paintings of animals in bright colours are very popular. The museum also has a nice cafe, called Kaya, after Kumagai's daughter, on the ground floor.

352 **TARO OKAMOTO MEMORIAL MUSEUM**
6-1-19 Minami-
Aoyama
Minato-Ku ④
+81 (0)3-3406-0801
taro-okamoto.or.jp

"Art is an explosion!" Taro Okamoto will forever be remembered for this quote and *The Tower of the Sun* in Osaka. This small museum displays many of the artist's works. It also has an excellent cafe, called Piece of Cake, where you can eat and drink while you admire his sculptures.

353 **THE NURIE MUSEUM**
4-11-8 Machiya
Arakawa-ku
+81 (0)3-3892-5391
nurie.jp

This museum exhibits colouring books from overseas and Japan but mainly focusses on the works of Kiichi Tsutaya, whose colouring books took Japan by storm from around 1945 to 1955. Japan's *kawaii* culture has its roots in his pictures. There is also a space where you can colour pictures. Have fun!

354 THE SHOTO MUSEUM OF ART

2-14-14 Shoto
Shibuya-ku ⑦
+81 (0)3-3465-9421
shoto-museum.jp

This art museum is located in a quiet residential area called Shoto. While the museum has no collection of its own, they do host amazing small exhibitions. Head over to one of the many places nearby after your visit as the museum has no cafe. Definitely a must-see during your stroll through Shibuya.

355 YAYOI MUSEUM

2-4-3 Yayoi
Bunkyo-ku ⑩
+81 (0)3-3812-0012
yayoi-yumeji-museum.jp

This museum has an extensive collection of book illustrations, including works by Kiyokata Kabyraki and Junichi Nakahara. The Takehisa Yumeji Museum next door exhibits the works of Takehisa, an artist whose work is representative of the Taisho period. The museum shop has a nice collection of original items.

5

UNUSUAL MUSEUMS

356 **SUGINAMI ANIMATION MUSEUM**
AT: SUGINAMI KAIKAN, 3RD FL.
3-29-5 Kamiogi
Suginami-ku
+81 (0)3-3396-1510
sam.or.jp

A museum for die-hard anime fans where they can learn more about anime history and enjoy old anime movies. The permanent exhibition includes recreations of the works of well-known animators. The museum also hosts anime workshops for kids where they can create their own. Check out the autographs of the many manga artists and voice actors near the entrance to the third floor.

357 **TOKYO SOME MONOGATARI MUSEUM**
3-6-14 Nishi-Waseda
Shinjuku-ku ⑪
+81 (0)3-3987-0701

This museum is located in Tomita Senkogei, a kimono workshop. They have been dyeing textile here since the Meiji period. The exhibits feature tools used for dyeing. The museum also organises workshops where you can learn to make *Edo Komon*, or stencil patterns.

358 PAPER MUSEUM

AT: ASUKAYAMA PARK
1-1-3 Oji
Kita-ku
+81 (0)3-3916-2320
papermuseum.jp

This museum, which opened in 1950, collects and exhibits documents on Japanese handmade washi paper and paper that was made overseas. Learn more about papermaking, paper recycling, and the history of *washi* and other handmade papers. The garden is just as instructive as it is full of plants that are used for papermaking.

359 PRINTING MUSEUM

1-3-3 Suido
Bunkyo-ku ⑩
+81 (0)3-5840-2300
printing-museum.org

One of the largest printing companies in Japan, called Toppan Printing, founded this museum in 2000 to commemorate its centenary. It is dedicated to the history and techniques of printing and also hosts temporary exhibitions of beautiful books and posters.

360 MEGURO PARASITO-LOGICAL MUSEUM

4-1-1 Shimo-Meguro
Meguro-ku ⑭
+81 (0)3-3716-1264
kiseichu.org

Biologist Satoru Kamegai created this museum, which hosts exhibitions about parasitic insects and conducts research on them. Unless you are an expert in this field, every display has new surprises in store for you. A rather unique museum.

メダマイカリムシ

鯖き魚の眼の中に
入れて寄生する中脳類

5 must-do's at
KOKUGIKAN

Kokugikan Stadium
1-3-28 Yokoami
Sumida-ku ⑮
+81 (0)3-3623-5111
sumo.or.jp

361 **GREET RIKISHI**

Would you like to see *rikishi* (sumo wrestlers) up close? Then wait for them near the west entrance. Only *yokozuna* and *ozeki*, the two highest ranks, can use cars to get to Kokugikan (so you are unlikely to see them). The *rikishi* of other ranks must walk there. Be there around 2 pm.

361 RIKISHI

362 EAT CHANKO AND YAKITORI

Rikishi eat *chanko*, a type of soup. The recipes vary, depending on the schools or the cooks. During tournaments, the schools take turns serving their *chanko* in the basement. *Yakitori* (grilled chicken skewers with a soy-based sauce) are probably the most famous snack at this venue.

363 VISIT SUMO MUSEUM

You can visit this museum if you have a ticket to a tournament. Learn everything there is to know about *sumo*, and in particular about its history. The exhibit changes every two months so visitors have good reason to return.

364 TAKE PURIKURA

Purikura, aka Print Club, is a unique photo booth where you can create your own photo stickers to take home as a souvenir. At Kokugikan, you can create a sheet of stickers of you and the *yokozuna* (and your friends as long as all of you fit in the booth).

365 BUY GOODS

There are several shops in Kokugikan. And some of the staff are larger than life. These retired *rikishi* now work for the Sumo Association as shop assistants. Some of the original merchandise is very practical, such as the *tenugui* (hand towel) and notebooks.

5 essential places for
MANGA and ANIME
LOVERS

---

366 DICE IKEBUKURO

1-11-11 Higashi-
Ikebukuro
Toshima-ku ⑪
+81 (0)3-5944-9202
diskcity.co.jp

DiCE Ikebukuro is the largest *manga kissa*, which is similar to an Internet cafe, in Tokyo. They stock about 180.000 manga titles on eight floors. Like Internet cafes, they have PCs, shower rooms, and bars. They even have an ice-cream machine (can be used without additional charge!) and a karaoke facility.

367 JUMP SHOP

AT: TOKYO DOME CITY
1-3-61 Koraku
Bunkyo-ku ⑩
+81 (0)3-5842-6844
*shonenjump.com/j/
jumpshop*

The shop of the Shonen Jump manga magazine. You can buy a variety of items illustrated with popular characters as well as comics. Some of them are only available from this shop. The shop's character Junta was created by Akira Toriyama, the creator of *Dragon Ball*.

368 KITARO CHAYA

5-12-8 Jindaiji
Motomachi
Chofu-shi
+81 (0)42-482-4059

Ge GE Ge no Kitaro is a popular manga and anime series, which was created in 1960. The characters of the series welcome you in the cafe where you can enjoy an original menu. See illustrations by the series' author, Shigeru Mizuki, on the second floor.

369 TOKIWASO-DORI OYASUMIDOKORO
2-3-2 Minami-Nagasaki
Toshima-ku ⑪
+81 (0)3-6674-2518

Tokiwaso is a block of flats that was built in the fifties and demolished in 1982. Several famous manga artists, such as Osamu Tezuka, Fujio Fujiko (both of them), Shotaro Ishimori, and Fujio Akatsuka lived here. Now there is just a monument to remind you that the building once stood here. You can still visit many of the places frequented by the artists in the area.

370 NAKANO BROADWAY
5-52 Nakano
Nakano-ku ⑫

A must-see if you want to experience Tokyo's subculture. Here you can find newly-published manga in rare first editions as well as figures and trading cards. You may find collectibles of anime characters that you used to watch on TV when you were a kid. Very pricy.

370 NAKANO BROADWAY

5 **SPOTS** *you may have seen in* **FILMS**

---

371 **JOUGANJI TEMPLE**
   2-26-6 Honcho
   Nakano-ku ⑫
   +81 (0)3-3372-2711
   nakanojouganji.jp

This is the temple Charlotte, played by Scarlett Johansson, visits when wandering around Tokyo in Sofia Coppola's *Lost in Translation*. This photogenic temple was built approximately 650 years ago. Spring is probably the best season to visit as there are weeping cherry trees on either side of the gate.

372 UENO PEDESTRIAN DECK

372 UENO PEDESTRIAN DECK

NEAR UENO STATION
Taito-ku ⑩

This place was featured in James Mangold's *The Wolverine*. Logan, played by Hugh Jackman, and Mariko, played by TAO, catch the bullet train to Osaka here. In reality, the trains to Osaka depart from Tokyo Station, not Ueno.

373 THE CREST TOWER

2-11-6 Tsukuda
Chuo-ku ⑮

In Alejandro González Iñárritu's *Babel*, Chieko Wataya, a deaf Japanese teenage girl played by Rinko Kikuchi, lives in a high-rise apartment with her father. Their apartment was in this building. Many similar high-rise buildings were built in this area in recent years.

374 SUGA SHRINE

5 Sugacho
Shinjuku-ku ⑤
+81 (0)3-3351-7023
sugajinjya.org

Seichi junrei, literally meaning 'pilgrimage', is a term that is mainly used by anime fans who like to visit the places that are featured in their favourite manga. This shrine was shown in an anime called *Your Name.* (Japanese title: *Kimi no Na wa*) by Makoto Shinkai. As the film became a blockbuster hit, many people have since visited the place to 'worship' it.

375 YANAGIBASHI BRIDGE

NEAR ASAKUSABASHI STATION
Higashi-Nihonbashi,
Chuo-ku ⑮
Yanagibashi, Taito-ku

Yanagibashi is a bridge over the Kanda River, just before its confluence with the Sumida River. This bridge was featured in the Japanese horror film *The Grudge* by Takashi Shimizu. The university professor Peter sees it from the balcony. This bridge is also a familiar feature in TV dramas.

The 5 most interesting
FESTIVALS
to catch

---

376 SANJA MATSURI

AT: ASAKUSA SHRINE

**2-3-1 Asakusa
Taito-ku** ⑩
+81 (0)3-3844-1575
asakusajinja.jp

This *matsuri* (festival) takes place every year in May at the Asakusa Shrine, which is also called Sanja-sama, one of the most famous Shinto shrines in the city. During the festival, portable *mikoshi* (miniature shrines) are carried around in processions by the neighbourhood associations in honour of the three founders of the Sensoji Temple.

377 KAGURAZAKA MATSURI

**Kagurazaka area
Shinjuku-ku**

In July, Awa-odori dancers flood the streets of Tokyo, in a frenzied spectacle as they parade through Kagurazaka. This is a great opportunity to experience this traditional area of the city. One of the verses of the song to which they dance says: 'A dancing fool and a watching fool. If both are fools, then you're better off dancing'. Fancy a dance?

378 TOUROU NAGASHI
Asakusa area
Taito-ku
+81 (0)3-3844-1221

In mid-August, during *O-bon* (one of the Buddhist rituals), we release candle-lit lanterns into the Sumida River to commemorate the souls of the people who died in the Sumida River during the Great Kanto Earthquake and the Great Tokyo Air Raids. Everyone can buy a lantern to join.

379 FUKAGAWA HACHIMAN MATSURI
AT: TOMIOKA HACHIMANGU SHRINE
1-20-3 Tomioka
Koto-ku ⑮
+81 (0)3-3642-1315
tomioka
hachimangu.or.jp

This is one of the three festivals in Tokyo that takes place around 15 August, and the most important event at the shrine. During *Hon-matsuri*, which takes place once in every three years, you can see a procession of 120 *mikoshi* or portable shrines. A few of the *mikoshi* are decorated with real gold and diamonds. Worth seeing!

380 AZABU JUBAN SUMMER NIGHT FESTIVAL
Azabu Juban area
Minato-ku ⑥

Every year in August. Though it was scaled down a few years ago, this festival still attracts a great many visitors. The area is known to have a variety of excellent restaurants, and these restaurants have stalls at the festival to offer their specialities at reasonable prices.

5
FIREWORKS
festivals not to miss

---

381 ADACHI NO HANABI
ADACHI FIREWORKS
FESTIVAL
**Riverbed of the
Arakawa River
Adachi-ku**

Every year in July the fireworks festival season kicks off with this festival. They launch around 12.000 fireworks over an hour, ending with 'Niagara', a fireworks display in the shape of a waterfall. Head to Nishi-Ari for a breath-taking view of the Niagara.

382 EDOGAWA HANABI TAIKAI
EDOGAWA FIREWORKS
FESTIVAL
**Riverbed of the
Edogawa River
Edogawa-ku**

The festival is also called 'Exciting Fireworks Festival' and it takes place in August. It begins with a jaw-dropping spectacular of 1000 fireworks, that are launched in just five seconds (yes, that's right, five seconds) followed by special displays, which change every year. This festival is the biggest crowd-puller.

383 ITABASHI HANABI TAIKAI
ITABASHI FIREWORKS
FESTIVAL
**Riverbed of the
Arakawa River
Itabashi-ku**
itabashihanabi.jp

This festival is held in August in collaboration with Toda City, Saitama, which is located on the opposite side of the river. About 12.000 fireworks are fired into the sky, making for a good show. There are some paid seats if you want to be certain that you'll have a good view.

384 SUMIDAGAWA HANABI TAIKAI

SUMIDAGAWA FIREWORKS FESTIVAL

Riverbed of the Sumida River Sumida-ku/Taito-ku
sumidagawa-hanabi.com

This festival was first organised in 1733. It is divided into two areas, and the sky is ablaze with dazzling colour from around 22.000 fireworks. A fireworks competition is held in one of the areas, with ten groups competing every year. Avoid the crowds by buying a ticket for a sightseeing boat to enjoy the spectacle from the water.

385 JINGU GAIEN HANABI TAIKAI

JINGU GAIEN FIREWORKS FESTIVAL

Jingu Gaien area Kasumigaokamachi/ Shinjuku-ku ④
jinguhanabi.com

The first festival was held in 2011 to raise funds in the wake of the Great East Japan Earthquake and since then it has been organised in August every year. Live music concerts, with a line-up of twenty bands, are held at the two baseball stadiums. Don't forget to buy tickets.

385 JINGU GAIEN HANABI TAIKAI

5 *great* **LIVE BARS** *and*
NIGHTCLUBS

---

386 **UNIT**
AT: ZA HOUSE BUILDING
1-34-17 Ebisu-Nishi
Shibuya-ku ②
+81 (0)3-5459-8630
unit-tokyo.com

They host club events and gigs here almost every night and are known for their excellent sound system. With plenty of legendary events in recent years, with musicians and DJs from Japan and overseas, this is the place to go if you want to enjoy an epic night.

387 **HARETARA SORANI**
MAME MAITE
AT: MON CHERI
DAIKANYAMA B2
20-20 Daikanyamacho
Shibuya-ku ②
+81 (0)3-5456-8880
haremame.com

This shop's long name means 'throw beans into the sky on a clear day,' but people usually call it Haremame'. They invite various musicians and DJs to give concerts here: some are well-known, even outside Japan, and others are from overseas.

388 **WWW**
AT: RISE BUILDING
13-17 Udagawacho
Shibuya-ku ①
+81 (0)3-5458-7685
www-shibuya.jp

This building used to be a cinema, which is why it has a multi-level floor. There is always something exciting going on, whether a gig by a young Japanese indie band or a performance by world-renowned jazz musicians. They also invite DJs and small theatre groups sometimes.

389 **SOUP**
AT: MIKASA BUILDING
3-9-10 Kami-Ochiai
Shinjuku-ku ⑫
+81 (0)3-6909-3000
ochiaisoup.com

Located in the basement of a bath house in a quiet residential area. This place only admits 100 people so the atmosphere is friendly. Do look for the bath house and launderette, and go down the stairs of the same building.

390 **AOYAMA HACHI**
AT: AOYAMA BUILDING,
2ND-4TH FL.
4-5-9 Shibuya
Shibuya-ku ①
+81 (0)3-5766-4887
aoyama-hachi.net

They have three DJ floors and a lounge bar on the fourth floor with a nice selection of music events including house and techno as well as soul, jazz, and reggae. The stylish atmosphere and excellent sound system attract huge crowds and world-famous DJs.

MiRAIKAN

25 THINGS TO DO
WITH CHILDREN

---

5 PARKS *that charge no admission* ——————— 210

5 *nice* ZOOS *and* AQUARIUMS ——————— 212

5 *great children's* BOOKSHOPS ——————— 214

5 *places for kids on* A RAINY DAY ——————— 216

5 SHOPS *and* SHOPPING CENTRES
where kids can spend hours ——————— 218

5
PARKS
that charge no admission

---

391 RINSHI NO MORI PARK

5-chome, Shimo-Meguro
Meguro-ku ⑭
+81 (0)3-3792-3800
tokyo-park.or.jp

This park was used as an experimental forestry station until the late seventies and reopened as a park in 1989. This explains why there are so many trees including rare trees, like the handkerchief tree, and rare plants, such as the native dandelion called *Kanto tampopo*.

392 TODOROKI KEIKOKU PARK

1-22, 2-37/38 Todoroki
Setagaya-ku ⑬

This park was designated a site of scenic beauty by Tokyo's Metropolitan Government. It is just a short walk from the nearest station, Todoroki. As you walk down the trail, you will forget that you are in busy Tokyo.

393 SAKURAZAKA PARK

AT: ROPPONGI HILLS
Roppongi
Minato-ku ⑥
roppongihills.com

This park is also known as 'Robo Robo Koen' as you can run into robots, which were created by the Korean artist Choi Jeonghwa, here and there. The park is best known for its tower of 44 robots and its slides. Don't look any further if your kids love to play.

394 TONERI IKIKI PARK

6-3-1 Toneri
Adachi-ku

Many of the features in this park were inspired by Japanese folk tales. The slope features a red demon and kids come out of the demon's mouth – very interesting. It is rather a small park, but it has a lot of stories (literally), and unique.

395 KINUTA PARK

1-1 Kinuta Koen
Setagaya-ku ⑬

There is an art museum, a bird sanctuary, and an athletics facility on site. This family park also has nice lawns with cherry trees. An excellent place for a picnic perhaps?

392 TODOROKI KEIKOKU PARK

5 nice
ZOOS and AQUARIUMS

396 INOKASHIRA PARK ZOO

1-17-6 Gotenyama
Musashino-shi
+81 (0)42-246-1100
tokyo-zoo.net/zoo/ino

Inokashira Park Zoo occupies approximately one third of Inokashira Park. This zoo is home to over 200 species, some of which are not kept in cages but in enclosures, like the squirrels. The park also has a duck sanctuary and breeds mandarin ducks which it releases into the wild.

397 UENO ZOOLOGICAL GARDENS

397 UENO ZOOLOGICAL GARDENS

9-83 Ueno Koen
Taito-ku ⑩
+81 (0)3-3828-5171
tokyo-zoo.net/zoo/ueno

Japan's oldest zoo opened in 1882 and attracts more than 3.000.000 visitors annually, who come to see 500 species of animals including a giant panda. Each animal is kept in an enclosure that replicates the environment they would usually live in. Ducks and sea gulls like to stop in the natural pond.

398 SHINAGAWA AQUARIUM

3-2-1 Katsushima
Shinagawa-ku ⑭
+81 (0)3-3762-3433
aquarium.gr.jp

One of the popular features of this aquarium is a tunnel tank that simulates the environment of Tokyo Bay. You will be amazed by how many creatures actually populate the bay. Enjoy a 360-degree panoramic view of the seals as they swim through the tank tunnel.

399 SUNSHINE AQUARIUM

3-1-1 Higashi-
Ikebukuro
Toshima-ku ⑪
+81 (0)3-3989-3466
sunshinecity.co.jp/
aquarium

This bright and airy aquarium is actually located on the building's rooftop. Here you can see penguins swim overhead and get close to several water animals. Check the feeding times for the penguins, pelicans, seals, and other animals.

400 SUMIDA AQUARIUM

AT: TOKYO SOLAMACHI
1-1-2 Oshiage
Sumida-ku ⑮
+81 (0)3-5619-1821
sumida-aquarium.com

This aquarium is located on the fifth and sixth floors of Tokyo Solamachi. See beautiful goldfish swim in the Edorium, including 'ordinary' goldfish (ryukin and wakin) as well as roundfish (ranchu). Take a look behind the scenes and learn more about the keepers' jobs in the Aqua Lab.

5 great children's
BOOKSHOPS

---

401 BOOK HOUSE CAFE

2-5-3 Kanda Jinbocho
Chiyoda-ku ⑨
+81 (0)3-6261-6177
bookhousecafe.jp

They call themselves a wonderland of picture books. Located in Jinbocho, or 'book town', they stock over 10.000 children's books. They also sell a selection of book-related goods for children, such as cuddly toys and stationary, and organise exhibitions of original artworks. They also have a cafe so you can spend all day here without having to worry about lunch.

402 BOOKS KYOBUNKWAN

4-5-1 Ginza
Chuo-ku ⑧
+81 (0)3-3561-8446
kyobunkwan.co.jp

This bookshop opened 120 years ago. In 1998, they added a children's section, called Narnia. The shop offers a range of around 15.000 titles, including popular older books and recent publications. They organise panel discussions and events. A cosy place for small children.

403 EHON HOUSE

1-7-14 Mejiro
Toshima-ku ⑪
+81 (0)3-3985-3350
ehon-house.co.jp

This shop sells imported picture books, mainly from European countries, including Germany, France, Italy, the Netherlands, and Sweden as well as English language learning materials for children. They also have a range of products inspired by children's books, like Moomin and Pippi Longstocking.

404 CHIE NO KI NO MI

2-3-14 Ebisu-Nishi
Shibuya-ku ②
+81 (0)3-5428-4611
chienokinomi-books.jp

The idea behind this bookshop's range is that parents want their children to read and love books. In addition to books, they also sell wooden toys that are child-proof. Parents and children can read together in the reading area on the second floor.

405 MIWA SHOBO

2-3 Kanda Jinbocho
Chiyoda-ku ⑨
+81 (0)3-3261-2348
miwa-shobo.com

This secondhand bookshop specialises in children's books. They have a wide range of picture books and children's literature, from Japan and other countries. They also sell a range of children's magazines from the 1950s and colouring books.

5 places for kids on
A RAINY DAY

406 TOKYO TOY MUSEUM
4-20 Yotsuya
Shinjuku-ku ⑦
+81 (0)3-5367-9601
goodtoy.org/ttm

This museum exhibits over 5000 toys from Japan and other countries in ten classrooms of a former primary school and is great fun for small children. They also have 10.000 toys that you and your kids can play with and a shop where you can buy gifts for children of all ages.

407 INTERNATIONAL LIBRARY OF CHILDREN'S LITERATURE
12-49 Ueno Koen
Taito-ku ⑩
+81 (0)3-3827-2053
kodomo.go.jp

One of the National Diet Libraries, which has a collection of over 10.000 children's books including 1800 titles in foreign languages. Learn more about the history of children's literature and picture books after the Meiji period in the second-floor gallery. The building, which was designed by Tadao Ando, is worth a visit.

408 ZUKAN MUSEUM
AT: TOKYU PLAZA GINZA, 6TH FL.
5-2-1 Ginza
Chuo-ku ⑧
zukan-museum.com

Zukan means a visual dictionary. This museum was founded by Japan's leading publisher Shogakukan, which publishes many dictionaries. A museum that will make you feel as if you've stepped into a dictionary that kids can enjoy while learning at the same time.

409 **MIRAIKAN**

2-3-6 Aomi
Koto-ku ⑮
+81 (0)3-3570-9151
miraikan.jst.go.jp

A great place to learn all there is to know about cutting-edge science and technology, with plenty of interactive displays. Even more enjoyable if you download the official app to your smartphone. On Saturdays, they don't charge admission for anyone under 18 (does not include the temporary exhibitions).

410 **SANRIO PUROLAND**

1-31 Ochiai
Tama-shi
+81 (0)42-339-1111
puroland.jp

An amusement park where you can meet the characters Sanrio created, such as Hello Kitty and My Melody. And what's more, you don't have to worry about the weather as this is an indoor park. Some of the merchandise they sell can only be bought here. If you are celebrating a birthday or another anniversary, you'll be treated to a bunch of fun specials.

409 **MIRAIKAN**

5 **SHOPS** and **SHOPPING CENTRES**

where kids can spend hours

---

411 **HAKUHINKAN TOY PARK**

8-8-11 Ginza
Chuo-ku ⑧
+81 (0)3-3571-8008
hakuhinkan.co.jp

This place is the stuff that kids' dreams are made of, selling everything from Barbie dolls to video games, on five floors. Check out the Hakuhinkan Racing Park on the fourth floor, where you can play with remote controlled cars. You may have to jostle for space with some grown-up kids though.

414 TOKYO CHARACTER STREET

412 YAMASHIROYA

6-14-6 Ueno
Taito-ku ⑩
+81 (0)3-3831-2320
e-yamashiroya.com

This popular toy store in Ueno has been here forever and sells various toys and party staples on six floors. Look out for their collectors' items, such as soft vinyl figures from classic TV series. Open until 9.30 pm.

413 AQUA CITY ODAIBA

1-7-1 Daiba
Minato-ku ⑮
+81 (0)3-3599-4700
aquacity.jp

Aqua City is a large 'entertainment shopping mall'. Here you'll find a toy shop and a 100 yen store, as well as Tokyo Leisure Land where you can take *purikura* and a shop where you can buy capsule toys. It also provides a place for children to nap.

414 TOKYO CHARACTER STREET

AT: FIRST AVENUE TOKYO STATION
1-9-1 Marunouchi
Chiyoda-ku ⑧
+81 (0)3-3210-0077
tokyoeki-1bangai.co.jp

In the underground shopping centre in Tokyo Station. The street is lined with shops of popular characters, including Hello Kitty, Rirakkuma, and Ultraman as well as the official shops of Tokyo's TV stations. They even have a shop where you can buy capsule toys from 100 vending machines.

415 TOKYO DOME CITY

1-3-61 Koraku
Bunkyo-ku ⑩
+81 (0)3-5800-9999
tokyo-dome.co.jp

A baseball stadium, amusement park, spa, restaurants, and a hotel in one location. ASOBono! is Tokyo's largest indoor facility and a great place for kids to use their imagination while playing.

HOTEL CHINZANSO TOKYO

20 PLACES
TO SLEEP

---

5 AFFORDABLE *accommodations* —————— 222

5 LUXURIOUS *hotels* ———————— 224

5 of the best BOUTIQUE *hotels* ————— 226

5 hotels that serve an
EXCELLENT BREAKFAST ————— 228

5

AFFORDABLE

accommodations

---

416 HOTEL VILLA FONTAINE TOKYO-KUDANSHITA

2-4-4 Nishi-Kanda
Chiyoda-ku ⑨
+81 (0)3-3222-8880
hvf.jp/kudanshita

Villa Fontaine is a budget hotel chain. Many people rely on this chain when travelling for business, as all their hotels are located in very convenient areas. The one near the Imperial Palace is an excellent choice for anyone who also wants to do some sightseeing in Tokyo. Each room is well-equipped.

417 TOKYO GREEN PALACE

2 Nibancho
Chiyoda-ku ⑤
+81 (0)3-5210-4600
tokyogp.com

This hotel is bright and clean and delivers good service at an affordable price. The breakfast buffet changes every morning so people can enjoy it even if they stay at the hotel for several days on end. They serve a lunch buffet on the weekends as well.

418 FIRST CABIN AKASAKA

3-13-7 Akasaka
Minato-ku ⑤
+81 (0)3-3583-1143
first-cabin.jp/hotels/
akasaka

This capsule hotel is a great option for anyone planning to visit several places using the Tokyo Metro. There are two classes of rooms: 'Business Class' and 'First Class.' The former is spacious by capsule hotel standards, while the latter is very roomy with a large storage box.

419 KANGAROO HOTEL

1-21-11 Nihonzutsumi
Taito-ku ⑲
kangaroohotel.jp

This stylish hotel, which offers good access to Ueno, Akihabara, and Asakusa, is a great option if you're travelling on a budget. Each room has a fridge and a TV. You'll find a microwave oven on each floor so that you can enjoy warm bento. You can rent a bicycle too!

420 NINE HOURS WOMAN SHINJUKU

2-13-7 Shinjuku
Shinjuku-ku ⑦
+81 (0)50-1807-3096
ninehours.co.jp/
womanshinjuku

This stylish capsule hotel is Japan's first wellness capsule hotel and is all about comfort, providing towels, slippers, a toothbrush, and something comfy to lounge in. Their '9h sleep fitscan' service analyses your sleep (you don't have to take them up on their offer). Sorry guys, this is female-only accommodation.

5
LUXURIOUS
hotels

421 HOSHINOYA TOKYO

1-9-1 Otemachi
Chiyoda-ku ⑧
+81 (0)50-3134-8091
hoshinoyatokyo.com

A luxury *ryokan* (Japanese inn) that offers you an extraordinary experience, just a 10-minute walk from Tokyo Station. The building is surrounded by several skyscrapers, and this contrast makes the hotel even more extraordinary. There is an open-air hot spring only for guests.

423 HOTEL CHINZANSO TOKYO

422 YUEN BETTEI DAITA

2-31-26 Daita
Setagaya-ku ⑬
+81 (0)3-5431-3101
uds-hotels.com/en/
yuenbettei/daita

Although just a half-minute walk from the nearest station, Yuen Bettei Daita provides respite from Tokyo's busy streets with its open-air bath and spa facilities. They also offer a day-trip plan with use of the bathing facilities and a meal. They also serve an amazing breakfast.

423 HOTEL CHINZANSO TOKYO

2-10-8 Sekiguchi
Bunkyo-ku ⑪
+81 (0)3-3493-1111
hotel-chinzanso-tokyo.jp

Chinzan literally translates as a 'mountain of camellias' as this place used to be a beauty spot where wild camellias grew. The hotel opened in 1992 on the site of the Chinzanso wedding centre. Guests can enjoy its gorgeous garden throughout the year.

424 IMPERIAL HOTEL

1-1-1 Uchisaiwaicho
Chiyoda-ku ⑧
+81 (0)3-3504-1111
imperialhotel.co.jp

The hotel is as Japanese as it gets. Opened in 1890, this was the first hotel to offer a laundry service and buffet-style restaurant in Japan. In Japan, an all-you-can-eat buffet is often called *baikingu*, or Viking. The president of the hotel at that time was inspired to call it like that by a scene in the film *The Vikings*, in which a band of Vikings attack their food with gusto.

425 THE PENINSULA TOKYO

1-8-1 Yurakucho
Chiyoda-ku ⑧
+81 (0)3-6270-2888
tokyo.peninsula.com

Needless to say, this hotel belongs to the chain of Peninsula Hotels. Since its opening in 2007, the hotel has received five stars in the Forbes ranking and several other awards. The guest rooms are decorated with natural wood in a distinctive Japanese style. The restaurants facing the Imperial Palace are an excellent choice for lunch.

5 of the best
BOUTIQUE
hotels

426 TRUNK (HOTEL)

5-31 Jingumae
Shibuya-ku ③
+81 (0)3-5766-3210
trunk-hotel.com

Opened in 2017, and located between Shibuya and Harajuku, this hotel inspired a new trend in Japan's hotel industry. This is not just a hotel. Calling itself a 'hotel for socialising', it has a bar lounge and restaurants where you can do just that.

427 MUSTARD HOTEL SHIMOKITAZAWA

3-9-19 Kitazawa
Setagaya-ku ⑬
+81 (0)3-6407-9077
mustardhotel.com/
shimokitazawa

From the outside, this place does not look like a hotel. But the Mustard, which opened in 2021, has a unique feature: every room has an old school record player and you can rent a selection of vinyl, from hip-hop to city pop, from the hotel's library.

428 LYURO TOKYO KIYOSUMI

1-1-7 Kiyosumi
Koto-ku ⑮
+81 (0)3-6458-5540
thesharehotels.com/
lyuro

This hotel also opened in 2017 in Kiyosumi Shirakawa. This area has popped up on everyone's radar because of the many organic cafes and restaurants that opened here in recent years. Some of the rooms have a 'River View bath', where you can enjoy a relaxing time gazing at the Sumida River.

429 **WIRED HOTEL**

2-16-2 Asakusa
Taito-ku ⑩
+81 (0)3-5830-7931
wiredhotel.com

Another 'wabi-sabi modern' hotel that opened in 2017. They have several types of rooms, including a dorm-style room and more luxuriously appointed ones. All the rooms, including the dormitory, have been kitted out with Swedish top-quality brand Duxiana beds. In the cafe and bar Zakbaran, you can sample healthy desserts made with tofu.

430 **HOTEL S**

1-11-6 Nishi-Azabu
Minato-ku ⑥
+81 (0)3-5771-2469
hr-roppongi.jp/hotelS

Located between Roppongi Hills and the Nishi-Azabu crossing, this hotel is convenient for anyone interested in a taste of Tokyo's nightlife. Some of the rooms have organic soaps and other amenities that female guests will appreciate. There are 12 apartments designated for thosewho plan to stay for more than a month.

428 **LYURO TOKYO KIYOSUMI**

5 hotels that serve an
EXCELLENT BREAKFAST

431 SOLARIA NISHITETSU HOTEL GINZA

4-9-2 Ginza
Chuo-ku ⑧
+81 (0)3-6731-5555
solaria-ginza.
nishitetsu-hotels.com

These days everyone takes photos and videos when served 'Instagrammable' foods. At this hotel, you tuck into some gorgeous decorated fruit sandwiches. Go early, because they are firm believers in the 'first come, first served' rule. Their salad plate and smoothie are also excellent.

432 PALACE HOTEL

1-1-1 Marunouchi
Chiyoda-ku ⑧
+81 (0)3-3211-5211
palacehoteltokyo.com

Grand Kitchen on the ground floor serves breakfast for guests and non-guests on weekdays. Take your pick from the buffet 'Grand Kitchen Breakfast' or choose the 'Palace Morning' option that lets you add dishes to your breakfast buffet, such as eggs Benedict or pot-au-feu.

433 TOKYO STATION HOTEL

1-9-1 Marunouchi
Chiyoda-ku ⑧
+81 (0)3-5220-1111
tokyostationhotel.jp

As its name suggests, Tokyo Station Hotel is located in Tokyo Station. The Atrium guest lounge is located on the top floor and serves a breakfast buffet with 110 different dishes. Only for hotel guests, however, so why don't you consider spending a night at the hotel if you have a good appetite?

434 HILLTOP HOTEL

1-1 Kanda-Surugadai
Chiyoda-ku ⑨
+81 (0)3-3293-2311
yamanoue-hotel.co.jp

Many authors, such as Yukiko Mishima and Yashinari Kawabata, loved this hotel. They still serve the breakfast of choice of these authors. You can choose between a Japanese or western-style breakfast. The first one includes grilled fish, a Japanese omelette, seaweed, pickled plums, miso soup, porridge and more. Both options are a well-balanced way to start your day.

435 HOTEL NIWA TOKYO

1-1-16 Kanda
Misakicho
Chiyoda-ku ⑨
+81 (0)3-3293-0028
hotelniwa.jp

This modern hotel with a distinctive Japanese twist serves a breakfast buffet. Its salad bar has a selection of over 20 different fresh vegetables, which it sources directly from contract farms. Egg dishes are cooked to order. You can also enjoy a seasonal vegetable soup, and a bowl of rice and miso soup.

WAKASU SEASIDE PARK

45 WEEKEND ACTIVITIES

5 *destinations for* A ONE-DAY TRIP FROM TOKYO ——————— 232

5 WEEKEND ESCAPES ——————— 234

5 *nice* RUNNING TRAILS ——————— 236

5 PUBLIC SWIMMING POOLS ——————— 238

5 HIKING / TREKKING TRAILS ——————— 240

5 CYCLING TRAILS ——————— 242

5 SPORTS FACILITIES
where you can relieve stress ——————— 244

5 FISHING SPOTS ——————— 246

5 FOOD FESTIVALS ——————— 248

5 destinations for
A ONE-DAY TRIP FROM TOKYO

436 **HAKONE**
Kanagawa

The trip from Shinjuku to Hakone by Odakyu Romance Car takes roughly 90 minutes. Hakone is known for its hot springs, but there are also several museums worth visiting. At Honma Yoseki Museum, you can observe how the craftsmen make beautiful wooden crafts called *Yoseki zukuri*.

440 MATSUMOTO CASTLE

437 SAKURA
Chiba

Just one hour from Tokyo Station and 30 minutes from Narita Airport, Sakura City is a residential suburb of Tokyo. It looks quite different from the capital however. Prepare to be amazed by the samurai's residences from the Edo period. Cycling around Inba Swamp can be fun.

438 HITACHINAKA
Ibaraki

Hitachinaka has a 200-hectare national park called Hitachi Kaihin Koen (aka Hitachi Seaside Park). The park is known for its flower gardens, attracting people all year round, even in winter! There are a few historical spots, including Hiraisho Hakuaso, a Mesozoic Cretaceous formation where you can find ammonites.

439 MISHIMA
Shizuoka

This city is located on the road to Mount Fuji from Tokyo. As the weather tends to be sunny here in winter, you may be able to admire beautiful snow-capped Mount Fuji. In May, you may spot fireflies in the area within walking distance of JR Station.

440 MATSUMOTO
Nagano

The perfect place for *soba* noodle lovers. Nagawa area, in Matsumoto, is known for its buckwheat and even has its own native variety. One of the main sightseeing spots is Nakamachi area, just a 10-minute walk from Matsumoto Station, with its typical black-and-white warehouses. Don't forget to visit Matsumoto Castle, which is a national treasure.

5

WEEKEND ESCAPES

441 CHICHIBU
Saitama

A good area for trekking. Mitsumine Shrine at the top of the mountain is considered to be one of the most sacred places in Japan. There is a natural hot spring and plenty of accommodation. After bathing, enjoy a cup of coffee brewed with spring water.

442 TATEYAMA
Chiba

Located in the south of Boso Peninsula, Chiba Prefecture, the trip here takes approximately two hours from Tokyo by express train. There are several beautiful beaches, that are especially popular in summertime. With seafood in abundance, this is a good place to enjoy excellent quality sushi.

443 IZU
Shizuoka

Hop on a bullet train at Tokyo Station, and you will arrive in Izu after just 45 minutes. The climate here is a moderate one. There are many hot springs in the area, and some of them are run like a public bath house: you can use them after paying a small fee.

444 **NIKKO**
Tochigi

Many people take a day trip to Nikko but there is loads more to see there. Canoe down the Kinugawa River and on Chuzenji Lake and go fishing in the Ojika River. You can stay at a *ryokan* with a hot spring.

445 **FUJI KAWAGUCHIKO**
Yamanashi

Four of Fuji's five lakes (Fuji Goko) are situated in Fuji Kawaguchiko. A place where you are guaranteed to have gorgeous views of Mount Fuji, in other words. Cherry blossoms in spring, lavender in summer, bright red foliage in autumn, and snow in winter… enjoy nature's splendour here throughout the seasons.

445 FUJI KAWAGUCHIKO

5 nice

RUNNING TRAILS

446 KOMAZAWA OLYMPIC PARK

**1-1 Komazawa Koen
Setagaya-ku** ⑬
+81 (0)3-3421-6431
tef.or.jp/kopgp

The 2,1-kilometre-long trail winds its way around the park, without traffic lights. It is more or less flat, and you can run while enjoying views of the park which change depending on the season. Near the park, there are a few facilities that let runners use their locker room.

449 ODAIBA KAIHIN PARK

447 MEIJI JINGU GAIEN

1-1 Kasumigaokamachi
Shinjuku-ku ④
+81 (0)3-3401-0312
meijijingugaien.jp

The road around Jingu Gaien is 1,3 kilometres long, but include Akasaka Imperial Gardens for a 3,3-kilometre run. There are a few shower facilities around the trail. One of them is a public bath house called Shimizu-yu (3-12-3 Minami-Aoyama, Minato-ku) which has towels and shampoo.

448 MEGURO RIVER

Nakameguro
Meguro-ku ②

A five-kilometre trail. The river is a popular spot for cherry blossom viewing from late March to early April. Runners are welcomed at the Kohmeisen public bath house (1-6-1 Kami-Meguro, Meguro-ku). There is even an open-air bath on the rooftop.

449 ODAIBA KAIHIN PARK

1-4 Daiba
Minato-ku ⑮
+81 (0)3-5500-2455

There are two trails in the park, of five and seven kilometres respectively. Both have a sea view, and are flat with no traffic lights, making this a perfect option for beginners. You can use the locker room and showers at Marine House near the start of the trail.

450 SHAKUJII PARK

1-26-1 Shakujiidai
Nerima-ku
+81 (0)3-3996-3950

The park has a 1,75-kilometre trail around Shakujii Pond. Unfortunately, there are no shower facilities in the park but you can use the coin-operated lockers at Shakujii Park Furusato Bunkakan next to the park. Though beautiful Sanpoji Pond (there are two ponds in the park) is not on the trail, it is definitely worth visiting.

5
PUBLIC
SWIMMING POOLS

---

451 AQUA FIELD SHIBA KOEN

2-7-2 Shiba Koen
Minato-ku ⑥
+81 (0)3-5733-0575
*minatoku-sports.com/
en/facilities/aqua.html*

There is a 50-metre-long pool as well as a futsal court. This outside pool is open from 1 July to 15 September. The depth of the pool changes depending on the time of the day. Remember: taking pictures or videos is strictly forbidden within the facility.

452 HAGINAKA PARK SWIMMING POOL

3-26-46 Haginaka
Ota-ku ⑭
+81 (0)3-3743-2155
haginaka.kbm.cc

This swimming centre, run by Ota City, has six pools. The outdoor pools are open from mid-July to the end of August, but the indoor pools are available throughout the year. From September to June, the pools are heated. There are indoor and outdoor water slides, so kids are bound to love this pool.

453 TOKYO GYMNASIUM

1-17-1 Sendagaya
Shibuya-ku ⑦
+81 (0)3-6380-4739
*tef.or.jp.e.apk.hp.
transer.com/tmg*

This gym was originally built for the Olympic Games in 1964. It has two indoor pools (25 m and 50 m), which are open throughout the year. You can buy a one-day pass to use both the swimming pools and the gym.

454 SUMIDA SPORTS KENKO CENTER

1-6-1 Higashi-Sumida
Sumida-ku ⑮
+81 (0)3-5247-7755
sumispo.com

Who cares about the weather when you can enjoy this fantastic indoor pool. There are five areas: a pool for infants and toddlers, a pool for children, a flowing pool, a 25-metre pool, and a water slide. On the 25th of every month, admission is free. Natural light flows into this indoor pool, making it a perfect place for a swim.

455 EAST CHOFU PARK POOL

5-13-1 Minami-
Yukigaya
Ota-ku ⑭
+81 (0)3-3728-7651
east-chofu.jp

Another swimming pool run by Ota City. The 25-metre indoor pool is open until 9 pm, but you can spend as much time as you want here. The outdoor pools are available in July and August. The 50-metre outdoor pool is usually less crowded than the other areas.

453 TOKYO GYMNASIUM

5
HIKING / TREKKING TRAILS

456 TAMA KYURYO
Hachioji-shi / Hino-shi / Tama-shi / Inagi-shi / Machida-shi

Tama Kyuryo is a vast area, extending from the border with Kanagawa Prefecture to the foot of Mount Takao. There are over 20 hiking trails in the area. One of the trails will lead you to the Sakuragaoka Rotary that was featured in Studio Ghibli's film *Whisper of the Heart*.

457 MOUNT JINBA
Hachioji-shi

This mountain (altitude: 857 metres) is located along the border of Hachioji City, Tokyo and Sagamihara City, Kanagawa. It is not difficult to climb, even for beginners. At the end of April, the mountain ridge is covered with cherry blossoms.

458 MOUNT ODAKE
Nishitama-gun

With an altitude of 1266 metres Mount Odake is one of the 200 highest mountains in Japan, where there are over 10.000 mountains. If you are not an advanced hiker, then use the cable car service. There are several hot springs around the mountain, don't forget to stop for a bath after your hike.

459 MOUNT TAKAMIZU
Ome-shi

This hiking trail winds its way along the ridge of three mountains: Takamizu (759 m), Iwatake Ishiyama (793 m), and Sogaku (756 m). It takes approximately four hours to walk the entire trail, making it suitable for beginners, including first-timers and primary school children.

460 MOUNT KAGENOBU
Hachioji-shi

This mountain is located between Mount Takao and Jinba. There are two traditional style tearooms (*chaya*) where you can enjoy beautiful views of Mount Fuji at the summit. If you take a bus from Takao Station and get off at Kobotoke, it takes about an hour to get to the summit.

5
CYCLING TRAILS

461 EDOGAWA CYCLING ROAD

BY THE EDOGAWA RIVER

Edogawa-ku

edogawacr.com

A 60-kilometre trail from the inlet of the Edo River to the point where it splits from the Tone River. Most of the trail is paved, so it is relatively easy for everyone. Please note the road is not for cyclists only, meaning you must always make way for pedestrians.

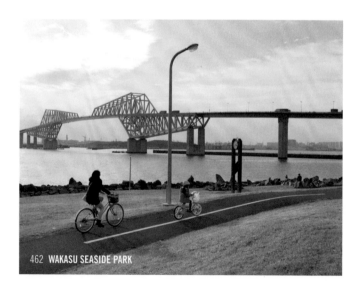

462 **WAKASU SEASIDE PARK**

462 WAKASU SEASIDE PARK

3-1-2 Wakasu
Koto-ku ⑮
+81 (0)3-3522-3225
tptc.co.jp/en/
c_park/03_07

This six-kilometre trail along Tokyo Bay is almost flat, making it the ideal course if you want to bike with your children. Rental bikes (26 inches and 20 inches) and tandem bikes are available. They also have animal-shaped bicycles and tricycles for children.

463 YOYOGI CYCLING CENTRE

2-1 Yoyogi
Kamizonocho
Shibuya-ku ⑦
+81 (0)3-3465-6855

Yoyogi Cycling Centre is located in Yoyogi Park. You can rent bicycles for adults and children as well as tandem bikes for two. There is an area where children can practise riding bikes with training wheels.

464 TAMAGAWA CYCLING ROAD
BY THE TAMA RIVER

Ota-ku ⑭

A 60-kilometre scenic trail along the Tama River. If you want to enjoy great views while cycling, this is a good choice. The trail runs past residential areas and public transport stations, so you can easily find toilets, vending machines, and convenience stores.

465 SHOWA MEMORIAL PARK

3173 Midoricho
Tachikawa-shi
showakinen-koen.jp

This park has a 14-kilometre cycling trail, and three 'cycling centres' where you can rent a bike. You can choose from 18 to 26-inches or rent a tandem bike. And naturally, you can also bring your own. This course is for cyclists only, no pedestrians allowed.

5

SPORTS FACILITIES

where you can relieve stress

---

466 ROCKY BOULDERING GYM

5-4-38 Konan
Minato-ku ⑭
+81 (0)3-6712-9538
rockyclimbing.com

The largest rock-climbing studio in Tokyo, which can accommodate up to 160 people. They have several courses that people of all levels can enjoy. Booking is not essential. Make sure to wear comfortable clothes for climbing and a pair of socks. You can also rent rock-climbing shoes.

467 B-PUMP TOKYO

1-1-8 Yushima
Bunkyo-ku ⑮
+81 (0)3-6206-9189
pump-climbing.com/gym/akiba

This is one of the largest bouldering facilities in the country, located just a five-minute walk from Akihabara station. The climbing wall on the fourth floor is in the roof-top area so you can feel the air and breeze as you make your way up the wall!

468 SPACE ATHLETIC TONDEMI HEIWAJIMA

1-1-1 Heiwajima
Ota-ku ⑭
+81 (0)3-6404-9935
bandainamco-am.co.jp/others/tondemi/heiwajima/facility-guide.html

This space has three floors of facilities, so you can enjoy wall climbing, trampoline, athletics, and running. As the facilities are run by BANDAI NAMCO Group, known for their game software, there is also an area where you can play games using your body instead of a game controller.

469 ASAKUSA BATTING STADIUM

AT: ROX DOME, 2ND FL.
1-27-5 Asakusa
Taito-ku ⑩
+81 (0)3-3485-5515
asakusa-bs.com

This batting range is located just a short walk from Sensoji temple. There are five batting cages, and one of them is equipped for both left and right-handers. You can adjust the speed of the ball from 70 to 150 km/h, so everyone can enjoy it, even first-timers.

470 OKURA LAND

3-24-1 Sakura
Setagaya-ku ⑬
+81 (0)3-3420-0271
okura-bowl.jp/
okuraland/index.html

This is an outdoor batting range within a recreational complex. Ball speed ranges from 80 to 120 km/h. Two of the six batting cages can also be used by left-handers. You can also play 10-pin bowling and practice golf here. Good to know: there is a restaurant on site so you could make a day trip of it.

5

FISHING SPOTS

---

471 BENKEI FISHING CLUB

**4-26 Kioicho
Chiyoda-ku** ⑤
+81 (0)3-3238-0012
*maidokun.com/
benkeifishing/*

Did you know that you can go bass fishing in Akasaka area? Fish from Benkei Bridge or hire a flyboat. There are carp and snakehead, and in winter, you might even pull up a rainbow trout. You can book a boat online for the weekends.

472 ICHIGAYA FISH CENTER

**1-1 Ichigaya Tamachi
Shinjuku-ku** ⑤
+81 (0)3-3260-1324
*ichigaya-fc.com/
fishing/*

Tsuribori is a leisure spot where you can enjoy fishing in an artificial pond. This *tsuribori* is located near Icjigaya Station, in the heart of Tokyo, where many people enjoy fishing for carp. There is a 'mini fishing' area, where small children can fish for goldfish and small carp.

473 KASAI RINKAI PARK

**6-2 Rinkaicho
Edogawa-ku
+81 (0)3-5696-1331**

There are a few fishing spots in this park, which faces Tokyo Bay. You can fish for gobies and bass throughout the year and some other fish depending on the season. Please note that surfcasting is not allowed here and there are plenty of stingrays, which have a venomeous sting of course.

474 THE EBITORI RIVER

**6-chome Haneda
Ota-ku** ⑭

The Ebitori River is a class A river near Haneda Airport. The name translates as 'prawn catching river' but you also catch gobies and young sea bass here. Bring your rod and other tackle as there is no shop nearby and a packed lunch if necessary.

475 YUMENOSHIMA GREEN PARK

**1, 2, 3-chome
Yumenoshima
Koto-ku** ⑮

In this park, which is only a three-minute walk from the nearest station, you can fish spiny gobies and bass for free. There is a fence on the bank, so you can let your kids fish with no worries.

BOAT HOUSE

471 BENKEI FISHING CLUB

5
FOOD FESTIVALS

476 AOYAMA PAIN FESTIVAL

AT: UNU FARMER'S MARKET

5-53-70 Jingumae Shibuya-ku ③

bread-lab.com

The most popular event at the UNU Farmer's Market. This festival lasts a weekend with more than 60 bakeries from all over the country participating every day. Some bakeries sell special sandwiches that were created just for this festival.

477 SHIMOKITAZAWA CURRY FESTIVAL

AROUND SHIMOKITAZAWA STATION

Setagaya-ku ⑫

curryfes.pw

Shimokitazawa is known for its small theatres, but it also has a few unique curry shops. At the festival, you can enjoy a 'curry stroll' from Indian and Thai curry to curry-flavoured *karaage* (fried chicken) and *omuraisu* (rice wrapped in a thin omelette), collect stamps each time you eat to get the limited edition T-shirt at the end of your stroll.

478 THAI FESTIVAL

AT: YOYOGI PARK

2-1 Yoyogi Kamizonocho Shibuya-ku ③

thaifestival.jp

This festival is organised by the Thai Embassy. With over 300.000 attendees every year, this is the most popular event in Yoyogi Park. From *tom yum goong* to *khao soi*, you can taste authentic Thai dishes as well as popular tropical fruit from Thailand.

479 CRAFT SAKE WEEK
craftsakeweek.com

The largest sake event in Japan, organised by ex-footballer Hidetoshi Nakata, takes place annually. During Craft Sake Week, selected sake brewers gather from all over the country to serve their sake. There are also stalls of well-known restaurants.

480 OKINAWA MATSURI
AT: YOYOGI PARK
2-1 Yoyogi
Kamizonocho
Shibuya-ku ③
okifes.tokyo

This festival promotes Okinawa, not just its food but also its music and traditional culture. Enjoy *goya champuru* (stir-fried bitter melon) and *mimiga* (pig's ear) while drinking an Orion Beer, and dance to *eisa* with friendly Okinawan people.

HACHIKO STATUE

20 RANDOM FACTS AND USEFUL DETAILS

---

5 things you should **NOT DO** in Japan —————— 252

5 **POPULAR MEETING SPOTS** —————— 254

5 things you should know before
GETTING ON A TRAIN —————— 256

5 facts about **JAPANESE TOILETS** —————— 258

5 things you should **NOT DO** *in Japan*

---

481 WEAR SHOES INSIDE THE HOUSE

You should take off your shoes before entering someone's house, a *ryokan*, or a temple's main hall unless you are told that it is not necessary. If there are slippers available, you should wear them instead. When visiting a temple in winter, take an extra pair of socks to ensure your feet stay warm.

482 BLOW YOUR NOSE LOUDLY

People in Japan don't like making noises except when they are eating noodles. If you need to blow your nose, use a paper tissue and both hands so you can do it quietly. In Japan, people do not use handkerchiefs to blow their nose.

483 KISS ON THE TRAIN, IN THE STREETS, IN A RESTAURANT, ETC.

Even if you wish to express your affection to your loved one who is sitting right beside you, don't kiss them in public. This is just not done in Japanese culture (though you may come across kissing couples later in the evening).

484 PLAY WITH CHOPSTICKS

There is such a thing as chopstick etiquette. Sticking chopsticks in a bowl of rice and passing food from chopsticks to chopsticks may be acceptable for non-Japanese people but Japanese people associate this type of behavior with funeral rites.

485 WASH YOUR BODY IN THE BATHTUB

If you go to a public bathing house or communal baths in a *ryokan*, you must wash your body before diving into the bathtub. Do not dip your towel or face flannel in the water. These rules are for hygiene purposes. You also prefer clean water in your bath, don't you?

5

POPULAR MEETING SPOTS

---

486 HACHIKO STATUE
OUTSIDE SHIBUYA
STATION (JR, TOKYO METRO)
1-2 Dogenzaka
Shibuya-ku ①

This is the statue of a legendary dog who was so loyal to his master that he used to wait for his master to come home in front of Shibuya Station even after he died. You might have seen Hachi in the film *Hachi: A Dog's Tale*, which was inspired by this dog's tale.

487 MOYAI STATUE
AT: SOUTH GATE SHIBUYA
STATION (JR, TOKYO METRO)
1-1 Dogenzaka
Shibuya-ku ①

While this may remind you of the statues on Easter Island, this statue comes from the Isle of Niijima which is a part of Tokyo. The name 'Moyai' comes from *moyau*, which is the island's dialect and means 'to cooperate'. The statues on the island were created about 50 years ago.

488 GIN NO SUZU SQUARE / SILVER BELL
AT: TOKYO STATION
Underground central
passage
Chiyoda-ku ⑧

This is supposed to be one of the popular meeting places at Tokyo Station, but you may find it very difficult to find as there are so many shops inside the station. Download the East Japan Railway app to your smartphone so you won't get lost.

489 **GODZILLA**

AT: HIBIYA CHANTER

1-2-2 Yurakucho

Chiyoda-ku ⑧

This three-metre Godzilla statue can be found in Hibiya Godzilla Square, which is in front of Hibiya Chanter. A convenient place to meet if you plan to visit Hibiya and Ginza areas. If you are a big fan of Godzilla, check out the other statue in the lobby of TOHO Cinema in Tokyo Midtown Hibiya.

490 **IKEFUKURO STATUE**

OUTSIDE IKEBUKURO STATION (JR, TOKYO METRO, SEIBU IKEBUKURO LINE, TOBU TOJO LINE)

Toshima-ku ⑪

Fukuro means 'owl' in Japanese but also sounds like *fu* (which is a prefix meaning 'no') and *kuro* (trouble). So *fukuro* is considered as a symbol of being free of trouble, without a hassle. *Fukuro* also rhymes with Ikebukuro. Ikefukuro is located near Kita-kaisatsu (the north ticket barrier).

489 GODZILLA

5 things you should know before
GETTING ON A TRAIN

---

491 DIFFERENT TICKETS FOR DIFFERENT TRAIN OPERATORS

There are several train operators on Tokyo's transport system: two subway operators, JR, and a few private railway companies. You must buy a ticket for each operator unless you have a special ticket for travelling on the trains of two connected operators. Consider buying a prepaid card, such as Suica or Pasmo.

495 LINE UP ACCORDING TO THE MARKS ON THE PLATFORM

492 PAY AT YOUR DESTINATION

Unlike many other countries, Japan allows people to adjust their fare at their destination. This means that you have a chance to pay the correct price at the end of the journey, even if you mistakenly bought a cheaper ticket. There are no plain-clothes ticket inspectors on board.

493 NO TALKING ON YOUR MOBILE PHONE ON THE TRAIN

Tokyo's train operators do NOT allow passengers to talk on the phone while on the train even though they have excellent reception. People just keep quiet and text. Do not forget to turn off the sound of your device either.

494 ESCALATOR ETIQUETTE – STAND LEFT

Nobody knows who decided this, but people stand left on the escalator in Tokyo (they do the opposite in Osaka by the way.) But do not walk or run on the right even if your train has arrived at the platform. Tokyo operates a frequent train service.

495 LINE UP ACCORDING TO THE MARKS ON THE PLATFORM

When you look at a platform, there are marks that tell you where the doors are. In other words, they tell you where you can get on the train. Usually, these marks make passengers queue in two lines. Sometimes, they also indicate the area where you can wait for the next train.

5 *facts about*

JAPANESE TOILETS

---

496 JAPANESE-STYLE TOILET

Japan has 'squat' toilets although they are few and far between nowadays as Western-style toilets are adopted more frequently in the home. Used toilet paper should always be flushed down the toilet – whether Japanese or Western.

497 RELATIVELY CLEAN

Even the public toilets in subway stations, in parks, or on the streets, are relatively clean. However, if you are a clean freak, carrying hand sanitiser with you is recommended as some of the public toilets do not have soap.

498 WASHLET

Washlet is a product invented by the Japanese company TOTO. If you press a button, a nozzle appears and washes your buttocks with lukewarm water. Please do not press the button when you are not sitting on the toilet.

499 OTOHIME

Japanese women do not like being heard when they use the toilet, so toilets have a machine that produces a flushing sound. If you don't mind this then don't bother using it. Be careful not to press an *otohime* button in error when you want to flush.

500 HOW TO FLUSH

There are plenty of different types. Push down handles, pull up handles, press buttons, sensors, automatic flushing toilets... It is complicated, even for Japanese people, so it must be even more difficult when you don't read Japanese. Look for a clue. Good luck.

INDEX

21_21 Design Sight 160
365 Nichi 64
3amours 96
3COINS 153
468 37
8ablish 80
Adachi no Hanabi 204
Akabana 92
AKOMEYA TOKYO
    in la kagū 125
And Wander 114
Angkor Wat 72
Aoba 50
Aoi 96
Aoyama Book Center 145
Aoyama Hachi 207
Aoyama Pain Festival 248
Aoyama Technical
    College 159
apéro. wine bar
    aoyama 97
Aqua City Odaiba 219
Aqua Field
    Shiba Koen 238
Archive Store 124
Asakusa
    Batting Stadium 245
Asakusa Culture Tourist
    Information Center 159
Au Bon Vieux Temps 135
Azabu Juban Summer
    Night Festival 203
B-Pump Tokyo 244
Bancho 74
Bar 5GALLON 92
bar à vin PARTAGER 96
BAR Uramen 93
Barbacoa 75
Benkei Fishing Club 246

Bépocah 75
Best Packing Store 124
Blue Brick Lounge 61
Bonjour Records 143
Book House Café 214
Books Kyobunkwan 214
Bouyourou 42
Bread, Espresso &
    Brown Rice 81
Bunkyo Civic Center 171
Café Paulista 103
Cando 152
Centre the Bakery 69
Cha Cha Kobo 99
Cha Cha no Ma 98
Cha-no-ha 99
Cherry Blossom 104
Cherry Brown 117
Chichibu 234
Chie no Ki no Mi 215
Chika Kisada 113
Citron 81
Cleansing Cafe 106
Coconut Glen's 63
Coffee L'ambre 102
CouCou 153
Craft Beer Market 95
Craft Sake Week 249
D&DEPARTMENT 127
D47 Shokudo 43
daidai 121
Daikanyama TSUTAYA
    Books 146
Daiso Harajuku 152
Daiwa Sushi 39
Daruma 71
David Otto 106
DiCE Ikebukuro 198
discland JARO 143

Disk Union 144
Dover Street Market
    Ginza 119
East Chofu Park Pool 239
Edogawa
    Cycling Road 242
Edogawa
    Hanabi Taikai 204
Ehon House 215
En Vedette 134
EVA 120
Face Records 144
Facetasm 118
First Cabin Akasaka 222
FLOTO 62
Fonda de la Madrugada 74
Food Truck Park 76
Francfranc 126
Fuchunomori Park 167
Fuji Kawaguchiko 235
Fujiiya 53
Fujimi Bridge 177
Fukagawa Hachiman
    Matsuri 203
Fukube 90
Fumito Ganryu 118
Gekkoso 149
Gin no Suzu Square 254
Ginza Six 131
Ginza 6-Chome
    Square Building 76
Ginza Tenryu 54
Godzilla 255
Gohyakurakanji 184
Golden Bagan 73
Gondola 135
Gostoso 74
Grill Swiss 55
Gyoza no Fukuho 53

Hachiko statue	254	Ikebukuro Station	174	Kimono Hazuki	122
Hagakure	57	Ikefukuro	104	Kinokuniya	
Haginaka Park		Ikefukuro statue	255	International	136
Swimming Pool	238	Imperial Hotel	225	Kinuta Park	211
Haibara	141	Inokashira Park Zoo	212	Kioi Small Hall	187
Hakone	232	International Library		Kisaburo Nojo	68
Hakuhinkan Toy Park	218	of Children's		Kissa You	68
Hamarikyu Gardens	168	Literature	216	Kitaro Chaya	198
Hana Chibo	82	Isetan Shinjuku Store	130	Kitchen Nankai	56
Hanahata Kinen Teien	169	Ishi no Hana	92	Kitchen Origin	77
Hands	128	Ishikawa Shuzo	172	KIYA	141
Haneda Airport	177	Isonoya (Iso-Zushi)	38	Koffee Mameya	101
Happo-en	168	Itabashi Hanabi Taikai	204	Kokugikan	
Harajuku Gyozaro	53	Ito-ya	148	Stadium	196, 197
Harajuku Gyozaro	53	Izu	234	Komazawa	
Hasegawa	91	Jalk Coffee	101	Olympic Park	236
Hassho	70	Japanese Ice Ouca	62	Kosoan	98
HIGASHIYA Ginza	180	JET SET Tokyo	143	Kumagai Morikazu	
Haretara Sorani		Jingu Gaien		Museum	191
Mame Maite	206	Hanabi Taikai	205	Kuon	35
Hikarie	130, 171, 180	Jiyugakuen		Kuri	91
Hilltop Hotel	229	Myonichikan	156	Kurumaya Bekkan	35
Hinomoto Brewing		Jouganji Temple	200	Kyo no Chiso	
& Beer Stand	95	journal standard		Hannariya	68
Hitachinaka	233	Furniture	127	Kyoeido	55
HMV & Books		JR Sobu Line	175	Kyourakutei	48
Shibuya	145	Jump Shop	198	La Collezione	160
Honke Abeya	42	Kabuki-za Theatre	186	Ladrio	102
Hoshinoya Tokyo	224	Kadan	79	Lemontea	121
Hotel Chinzanso		Kagurazaka Matsuri	202	Lilla Dalarna	78
Tokyo	225	Kakimori	149	Living Motif	127
Hotel Gajoen Tokyo	181	Kamawanu	142	Loft	149
Hotel Niwa Tokyo	229	Kameido		Lumine Ikebukuro	181
Hotel Ryumeikan		Gyoza Honten	54	Lyuro Tokyo	
Ochanomizu		Kameido Tenjin	185	Kiyosumi	226
Honten	224	Kameju	133	Maison de	
Hotel S	227	Kanda Coffee	101	Maruyama	124
Hotel Villa Fontaine		Kanda Matsuya	47	Maison Hermès	159
Tokyo-Kudanshita	222	Kangaroo Hotel	223	Mame Kurogouchi	112
HYKE	119	Kanno	39	Mandarin Oriental	180
Hyotan	71	Kanze Noh Theatre	187	Manganji Temple	
Ichigaya Fish Center	246	Kasai Rinkai Park	246	Todoroki Fudoson	184
IDÉE	127	Kasho Shoan	133	Mangetsu	37
Idemitsu		Kawachiya Shokuhin	137	Manmando	100
Museum of Art	189	Kawaguchi	91	Marunouchi	
Ikebukuro Seibu	130	Kikuura	35	Street Gallery	167

Maruzen 149
MASU 113
Matsumoto 233
Matsumotoro 56
Matsuneya 142
Matsuo 47
Meguro Parasitological
   Museum 194
Meguro River 237
Meiji Jingu Gaien 237
Meikyoku Kissa Lion 103
Menya Ishin 49
Menya Nukaji 49
Milonga Nueva 102
Miraikan 217
Mishima 233
Mitsubachi 63
Miwa Shobo 215
Miyagiyu 178
Miyakawa 45
Mizuho 132
Mochizuki 82
Momijiya 71
MONAKA Jewellery 117
Mont-Bell 114
Morioka Shoten 146
Mount Jinba 240
Mount Kagenobu 241
Mount Odake 240
Mount Takamizu 241
Mountain Research 115
Moyai statue 254
Mustard Hotel
   Shimokitazawa 226
Myojin-no-yu 178
Myojinshita
   Kandagawa 35
Nagi Shokudo 81
Nakano Broadway 199
Nanamica 114
Naniwaya 59
National Azabu 136
National Theatre 187
Natural House 77
Nezu Art Museum 188
Nihonbashi Brewery 95

Nikko 235
Nine Hours
   Woman Shinjuku 223
Numéro Cinq 97
Odaiba Kaihin Park 237
Ohitsuzen Tanbo 51
Okadaya 128
Okinawa Matsuri 249
Okonomiyaki
   Yamamoto 71
Okuno Karuta 141
Okura Land 246
Omotesando Hills 160
Omusubi Café 51
Onigiri Asakusa
   Yadoroku 52
Onigiri Bongo 51
Onigiriya Marutoyo 52
Ota Memorial
   Museum of Art 188
Oyama Kimono 122
Oyamada
   Ryokuchi Park 177
Ozawa Shuzo 173
Palace Hotel 228
Paper Museum 194
Pariya 76
Pignon 78
Prada 158
Premium SOW 62
Printing Museum 194
Quolofune 132
Rainbow Bridge 177
Ramen Jiro 50
Rebaya 57
Reversible Destiny
   Lofts – Mitaka 156
Rice Curry Manten 55
Rikugien Gardens 168
Rinshi no Mori Park 210
Rocky
   Bouldering Gym 244
Roppongi Hills 166
Ryan 61
Ryotei 156
Sakura 233

Sakurazaka Park 210
Samurai Rock 105
Sanbyakuya 58
Sanja Matsuri 202
Sanrio Puroland 217
Santokudo 59
Sarashina Horii 47
Satake 48
Saya-no-yudokoro 179
Seijo Ishii 136
Seikotei 135
Sekiguchi
   Catholic Church 157
Sen-Oku Hakukokan
   Museum 189
Seria 152
Setagaya Boro Ichi 122
Shakujii Park 237
Shibuya scramble
   crossing 174
Shibuya Station 161
Shigekuniya 55 Bakery 65
Shihara 117
Shimizuyu 179
Shimokitazawa
   Curry Festival 248
Shinagawa Aquarium 213
Shinjuku Gyoen
   National Garden 169
Shinjuku Horumon 58
Shinjuku Station 174
Shinjuku Suehirotei 187
Shirotae 135
Shizuoka SHIMBUN
   and Shizuoka
   Broadcasting
   System Building 157
Showa Memorial Park 243
Simmon 117
Sky Carrot
   Observatory 171
Sky High Daikanyama 107
Sky Lounge 171
Snow Peak 115
Solaria Nishitetsu
   Hotel Ginza 228

Sora to Mugi to	65	The Iceberg	159	Tsukiji Donburi Ichiba	38
soup	207	The Nurie Museum	191	Tsukiji Sushisay	36
Space Athletic Tondemi		The Peninsula Tokyo	225	Tsukiji Tama Sushi	36
Heiwajima	244	The Shoto		Tsunahachi	45
Spring Valley		Museum of Art	192	Tsutaya Electrics	125
Brewery Tokyo	95	THREE Revive		TWO ROOMS	
Stellar Garden	83	Kitchen Hibiya	81	Grill / Bar	82
Suga Shrine	201	Toa	129	T.Y. Harbor	94
Suginami Animation		Todoroki Keikoku Park	210	Ueno Pedestrian Deck	201
Museum	193	Tofuya Ukai	34	Ueno	
Sumida Aquarium	213	Toga XTC	120	Zoological Gardens	213
Sumida Sports		Tokiwaso-dori		UJOH	113
Kenko Center	239	Oyasumidokoro	199	UNDERCOVER	118
Sumidagawa Hanabi		Tokyo Art Museum	161	UNIT	206
Taikai	205	Tokyo		Unu Farmer's	
Sungari	79	Character Street	219	Market	138, 140
Sunshine Aquarium	213	Tokyo Dome City	219	Uogashi Meicha	98
Sunshine Juice	107	Tokyo Green Palace	222	Utou	91
Suragan	72	Tokyo Gymnasium	238	Velvet	120
Sushi Dai	38	Tokyo Hotarudo	123	View and Dining	
Sushi no Midori	36	Tokyo International		The Sky	83
Tachibana		Forum	167	Village Vanguard	146
Shinsatsushitsu	93	Tokyo Juice	106	Ville Marche	137
Ta-im	78	Tokyo Metro		VIRON	64
Talkative	166	Tozai Line	175	Wakasu Seaside Park	243
Tama Kyuryo	240	Tokyo Metropolitan		WIRED Hotel	227
Tamagawa		Government Building		WWW	206
Cycling Road	243	Observation Decks	170	Yakitori Moe	69
Tamagawa Sengen		Tokyo Midtown	167	Yamanoue	44
Shrine	176	Tokyo Port Brewery	172	Yamashiroya	219
Tamura Shuzojo	173	Tokyo Some Monogatari		Yamatane	
Tansuya	123	Museum	193	Museum of Art	188
Taro Okamoto		Tokyo Somei		Yanagibashi Bridge	201
Memorial Museum	191	Onsen Sakura	178	Yanmo	42
Tateyama	234	Tokyo Station Hotel	228	Yasukuni Shrine	184
Tea Cocktails		Tokyo Toy Museum	216	Yayoi Museum	192
at Mixology Salon	105	Tokyu Food Show	131	Yohei Ohno	113
Tenhide	44	Toneri Ikiki Park	211	Yoyogi Cycling Centre	243
Tenho	49	Toranoko	101	Yuen Bettei Daita	225
Tensaku	44	TORAYA	59	Yumenoshima	
Thai Festival	248	Tori Chataro	57	Green Park	247
Thailand	73	Tosa Dining Okyaku	43	Yukiguni	104
The Agnes Hotel &		Toshimaya Shuzo	172	Yuzawaya	128
Apartments Tokyo	228	Tourou Nagashi	203	Zenpukuji	185
The Crest Tower	201	TRUNK (HOTEL)	226	Zuien Bekkan	72
The Ebitori River	247	Tsuyose	129	Zukan Museum	216

COLOPHON

EDITING *and* COMPOSING — Yukiko Tajima

GRAPHIC DESIGN — Joke Gossé, Tinne Luyten and doublebill.design

PHOTOGRAPHY — Koji Ishikawa — koji-ishikawa.com

COVER IMAGE — Chidorigafuchi Park (secret 501)

The addresses in this book have been selected after thorough independent
research by the author, in collaboration with Luster Publishing. The selection
is solely based on personal evaluation of the business by the author. Nothing
in this book was published in exchange for payment or benefits of any kind.

D/2023/12.005/23
ISBN 978 94 6058 3490
NUR 510, 517

© 2018 Luster, Antwerp
Third edition, September 2023 – Third reprint, September 2023
lusterpublishing.com – THE500HIDDENSECRETS.COM
info@lusterpublishing.com

Printed in Italy by Printer Trento.